Art Licensing 101

SELLING REPRODUCTION RIGHTS TO YOUR ARTW(

ArtNetwork
Press

ART LICENSING 101, SELLING REPRODUCTION RIGHTS TO YOUR ARTWORK FOR PROFIT

Copyright © June 2002 by Michael Woodward

Cover and interior design by Laura Ottina Davis

Edited by Constance Smith

Published by ArtNetwork, PO Box 1360, Nevada City, CA 95959-1360
(800) 383 0677   (530) 470 0862   (530) 470 0256 Fax
www.artmarketing.com   <info@artmarketing.com>

ArtNetwork was created in 1986 with the idea of teaching fine artists how to earn a living from their creations. In addition to publishing art marketing books and newsletters, ArtNetwork also has a myriad of mailing lists available for rent. See the back of this book for details, visit u son-line or call our 800 number for a brochure.

The author, Michael Woodward, can be contacted at 1532 US 41 Bypass S #272, Venice, FL 34293-1032 941/488-8464 941/488-8454 Fax www.artlicensinginc.com   <artlicensing@comcast.net>

Publisher's Cataloging-in-Publication (provided by Quality Books Inc.)

Woodward, Michael.
    Art licensing 101: selling reproduction right to your artwork for profit /
    Michael Woodward. -- 1st ed.
        p. cm.
        Includes index.
        ISBN 0-940899-77-2

    1. Art--Marketing. 2. Copyright--Art. 3. License
    agreements. I. Title.

    N8600.W66 2002   706'.88
                      QBI02-200333

All rights reserved. No part of this book may be reproduced in any form or by any electronic or mechanical means including information storage and retrieval systems without permission in writing from the publisher, except by a reviewer, who may quote brief passages in a review.

DISCLAIMER: While the publisher and author have made every reasonable attempt to obtain accurate information and verify same, occasional address and telephone number changes are inevitable, as well as other discrepancies. We assume no liability for errors or omissions in editorial listings. Should you discover any changes, please write the publisher so that corrections may be made in future printings.

Printed and bound in the United States of America

FROM THE PUBLISHER

When I started in the art business some 20 years ago as an art rep in the San Francisco Bay Area, I knew nothing about the licensing and publishing industry. Though I had purchased a few posters, I didn't know "where they had come from." Looking back, I find that odd, yet, as I talk to artists today, I realize they know less than I did back then!

Most of the seminars I've given in the last several years have, by popular demand, been on this topic——publishing and licensing. The topic created so much interest at ArtExpo NY 2000 that there was a standing-room-only crowd of 500 people at a seminar on the subject. I knew then that it was a topic that needed to be addressed more thoroughly—in book format.

If you are marketing your original artwork, it could behoove you to learn about the licensing and publishing industry. It's a vast part of the art market.

In this book we've not only included how to approach the licensing and publishing marketplace, but we also have names of professionals working in that marketplace. The resource section has over 200 listings compiled from responses to questionnaires sent out to 3200 people in the industry. Along with all other miscellaneous reference sources, you will have all the information you need to make your licensing project a success.

A final word: if you don't own *Art Marketing 101* and *Art Office,* you are missing two necessary items to improve your art business. *Art Office* has many forms, letters and legal agreements that will come in handy for your long-term career. *Art Marketing 101* has over 300 pages of valuable information you need to know and understand about the art market.

I encourage you to **use** this book. Refer back to it. Keep it at hand. Write in the margins. Take notes. Put paper clips and Post-it notes on pages you'll need to refer to again.

I wish you the best of times with your career.

Constance Smith
Publisher and Editor

TABLE OF CONTENTS

CHAPTER 1   THE LICENSING INDUSTRY

CHAPTER 2   MARKETPLACES

CHAPTER 3   LEGAL ASPECTS

CHAPTER 4   BUSINESS PRACTICES

CHAPTER 5   PRESENTATIONS

CHAPTER 6   LICENSING AGENTS

CHAPTER 7   SELF-PUBLISHING PRINTS

CHAPTER 8   SELF-PUBLISHING CARDS

CHAPTER 9   HOME-GROWN CALENDARS

CHAPTER 10   CONTACTS

INDEX

DEDICATION

This book is dedicated to all artists—past, present and future—who enrich our lives through their artistic endeavors. I sincerely hope this book will help them improve their income and to enjoy a richer, fuller life, in what has become one of the most exciting industries on the planet. I hope in some small way my contribution will make a difference. I also dedicate it to Stewart, Neil, John and Ray—good friends no longer with us but not forgotten.

Michael Woodward

ACKNOWLEDGEMENTS

I'd like to thank Constance Smith, my publisher and editor who has labored long and hard editing my material and making significant contributions without which this book would have been incomplete. I would also like to thank Janet who encouraged me to start this project and who took on more than her fair share of work to give me the space to write.

INTRODUCTION

All you have to do is look around you. Our world is full of printed imagery. Licensing is a $175 billion industry. The industry has grown enormously since I first entered it in the early 70s. America has thousands of manufacturers and publishers, from greetings cards and fine art prints to furniture, pottery and children's apparel, all requiring art and design in some form.

This book is aimed at those artists who are serious about making money from their art. An artist considering a move into this industry needs to understand its foundations.

Licensing is granting licensees/publishers/manufacturers permission to use your work in return for a fee or royalty. If you want to make a better living, licensing can give you the opportunity to make $50,000 a year or more. The key to success in this industry is producing art with a wide range of appeal, which fits a particular market or product category.

WHAT WILL YOU LEARN?

You have in your hands the necessary tool and information to set in motion your own licensing program and increase your income substantially. To succeed, you will need 100% determination, perseverance and a degree of talent. There are no hard and fast rules to achieving success in this industry. I have represented artists who have earned $5,000 one year, $50,000 the next. Having licensed over $600 million of retail product through my company in the last 21 years, I have gained invaluable insights into this fascinating industry.

With this in mind, let's get started down the road to licensing success!

Michael Woodward

Chapter 1
The Licensing Industry

What is licensing?

How the market operates

Terminology

Royalties

Property sectors

Art and design sector

Art and design licenses

One must act in painting as in life, directly.
Pablo Picasso

WHAT IS LICENSING?

Licensing is granting the right to a licensee/publisher/manufacturer to reproduce your artwork on a particular product in return for a fee or royalty.

The licensing industry is a $175 billion industry, and growing. That is a huge increase from 20 years ago, when it was estimated to be a $10 billion industry worldwide.

Licensing is the business of leasing a copyrighted or trademarked "property," in this case a work of art, by means of a contractual agreement (a license), for a specific product (or promotion or service), for a specific time period, in an agreed upon territory, for an agreed upon fee or royalty.

Fine artists have the opportunity of enhancing their reputation by licensing their work of art for many products, including greeting cards, prints, posters, gift stationery, T-shirts, collector plates, furniture—literally hundreds of items. Licensing is an excellent way to build awareness nationally and internationally, thereby increasing the collectability of your art and hopefully the prices of your originals!

Licensing is now used extensively to create revenue streams for sport, fashion, entertainment, corporate brands, music, charities, publishing, games, celebrities, as well as the subject of this book—art and design.

Museums, many of which in the past frowned upon licensing as "too commercial," are now licensing art in their collections—Monet, Warhol and Mondrian, to name a few.

For an individual artist, the question is, "How can I introduce my work to the licensing marketplace?" This book will guide you through that process by showing you how to study the marketplace and how to create effective presentations that focus on specific products and potential licensees.

Artwork chosen by licensees (publishers and manufacturers) must have wide consumer appeal and stand up against the competition. Licensees are looking for that "extra something" in a work of art that gives it broad range consumer appeal. The higher the print or product run, the wider the appeal must be. The more product that is sold, the higher the royalties.

HOW THE MARKET OPERATES

The marketability of your artwork, or the product produced from your artwork, essentially has to bring a certain amount of revenue for commercial viability. The publisher makes a profit, the artist makes a royalty, the consumer is happy.

Marketability is one of the most fundamental and important facets of this business. You, the artist, must understand this fully to have any chance of success. You may produce some really innovative and radical new work. But is there a market? More importantly, does a publisher have a market for it?

Quite often you may be pitching this new artwork to the wrong publisher. You need to learn about each publisher's needs and who their customers are. You will also need to learn about what is selling in the market place. More importantly, you must learn what doesn't sell. A publisher will continue to use your work if it continues to sell. You will need to keep updated on what is happening in the sector of the industry you wish to target, by reading magazines and visiting trade shows and retail outlets.

➤ Respect requests of your licensee/publisher. They are assuming the financial risk of reproduction of your artwork.

➤ Don't change agents/licensors/publishers without a very good reason. It takes time to promote any given artist. If they are doing absolutely nothing, yet keep promising to, maybe it is time to change. Talk to them first.

➤ Work together—like butter and popcorn. Make efforts to help your agent/licensor/publisher. Visit their offices, offer some assistance. Send them a card on their birthday—maybe even to the accountant so they will pay your royalty checks on time!

BE FOREWARNED

➤ Are you overly protective of your work? Many publishers want to crop a piece; perhaps you do not want it cropped.

➤ Do not expect to have much involvement in the actual printing process. You can ask for certain rights, but ultimately the publisher will have rule here.

➤ Know why you are wanting to publish before you proceed. Is money your bottom line? Promotion? Publicity? Fame?

➤ Publishers might start suggesting what subjects to paint. Are you against commissions?

To learn more about the business, purchase copies of some of the magazines listed in the appendix. Decide which ones will help you the most in your business, then subscribe!

COMMERCIALISM

Despite the lure of making lots of money from licensing art, many fine artists are reluctant to jump into the business. A lack of industry knowledge, coupled with concern over damaging their status in the fine art market, can prevent an artist from pursuing a successful licensing career. What artists inevitably find out is that through licensing they can actually become much more recognized. If handled properly, licensing will actually enhance their reputation.

Running a business licensing your art is a commercial exercise to earn you a better living. Many artists forget this simple fact. While it is important to be creative and original, this must be tempered with ensuring that your work is commercially viable.

➤ Create your artwork in sets of a minimum of four images that "go together."

➤ Create your artwork in a 3:4 ratio that would fit a 9x12″ or 18x24″—two very common reproduction sizes—or 6x9″, a common book size.

STYLES AND THEMES

Style is very important to licensees/publishers/manufacturers. Some prefer traditional, some prefer contemporary styles; pastel, crayon, watercolor, oil, acrylic artworks are all used by licensees. They want to review only specific styles of art that fit into their product line. You will need to study each licensee's catalog to gauge what kind of work they use and the treatment thereof.

Another major factor is to establish a theme you can follow for a length of time. Some artists are versatile and can paint wildlifes, landscapes, seascapes, and even figurative work. You need to decide which market you are aiming for at the outset. Are you are considering the print industry? Do you want to establish a group of collectors, who, once they've bought a print, become collectors of your work and buy more? As your reputation grows, so does your market. If, however, you suddenly change your subject matter, say, from African wildlife to seascapes, even though the work may be exquisite, it confuses your buyer. Your collectors of African wildlife collect wildlife. Your publisher would have to begin anew, establishing a market for a seascape client-base.

Galleries often specialize too. If you have 100 galleries buying your African wildlife prints and you change to seascapes, then you might lose your entire gallery-base. The publisher then has to start over again to promote your new artwork—building a new gallery-base. Your royalties will probably be nonexistent for awhile, if you're lucky enough to even continue with the same publisher.

To create a collector base, stay with one subject and master it. When you have achieved a level of success, that's the time to experiment.

Artists who are aiming at greeting cards and gift stationery can afford to be a little more versatile. You will see quite clearly in card stores that if you establish a very strong style and theme, an entire section of a rack of cards can be devoted to your work. If the card range is successful, then this art can be used to create other gift products, thereby increasing your earning potential enormously.

It is important, then, to understand your personal "voice" in order to understand the market for which it will be appropriate. Define your work. What are you best at? What markets interest you? Visit retail outlets, department stores, galleries, frame shops—every outlet that sells the products you feel your work is best suited for. Take notes. Learn all you can about where your voice can fit.

TERMINOLOGY

In order to license your work, you have to think like a marketer or merchandiser. You need to understand consumers, their purchasing patterns and their desires.

BRAND

A product with a distinctiveness in its design or logo

FLAT FEE

A onetime fee (with no royalties) paid by a licensee for the use of artwork

GUARANTEES AND ADVANCES

A guarantee is the minimum monetary payment that the artist/licensor receives for the term of a given license. A guarantee is usually in the form of a nonrefundable advance, invoiced at the outset. Guarantees can also be in the form of a yearly minimum for each year of the license, provided the artist creates a specified number of designs each year. Example: A greeting card publisher wants an artist exclusively for cards. He may offer the artist a guarantee of $15,000 per year minimum for providing 50 card designs (against a royalty of 5% of sales).

INTELLECTUAL PROPERTY/PROPERTY

This is the "right" in a particular artwork or design (or trademark) that is owned by the artist or held in trust by an agent.

LICENSING AGENT

Licensing agents often specialize in a sector of the industry (see page 19 for definitions of sectors). They assume such duties as finding licensees, negotiating fees, issuing licenses, securing product approval, and the collection and accounting of fees and royalties received from product sales generated by the licensee.

Some licensing agents handle many properties, including trademarks such as Coca Cola or Harley Davidson, which are licensed to manufacturers for stationery, mugs, apparel and a host of giftware products, as well as TV properties such as The Simpsons, Rugrats, Sesame Street, etc. Art is often just one of many types of properties an agent might handle.

LICENSING CONSULTANT

Licensing consultants support manufacturers by aiding them in the evaluation of a property, developing the implementation of a licensing strategy, etc. Usually they work for the licensee on a commission basis. A consultant can also work for a licensor (owner of a property), a major artist, museum or the estate of a deceased artist, to help design a strategy to build a licensing program.

LICENSEE

A licensee is anyone, usually a manufacturer or publisher, who obtains permission from the owner/licensor or the owner's agent, for the right to use the property. The licensee then manufactures a specific product to sell in the marketplace to consumers.

LICENSOR

A licensor can be the artist or her agent who is authorized to grant licenses on the property (artwork).

MANUFACTURER

See Licensee above

PRODUCT DEVELOPERS

Product developers start with prototypes and follow through the assembly and packaging stages. They usually work for the manufacturer. There are, however, freelance specialists who produce innovative packaging ideas, which they sell to manufacturers.

PUBLISHER

See Licensee above. Usually prints posters, greeting cards, books.

SUB-LICENSE

If you agree to a clause allowing your licensee to "sub-license," you give permission to your licensee to license the art he has licensed from you (without any additional approval from you). Many manufacturers/ licensees now have their own licensing operations—this is a way that they can earn extra revenue. They will receive 50% of your royalty if they license your art for another product. This could cause you conflicts, as you may be actively licensing your work as well as the licensee. Avoid a sub-license in a contract at all costs, unless you particularly want the licensee to be your agent.

TRADEMARK

A trademark is any word, name or design (or combination thereof), usually in the form of a logo or unique symbol. To protect this design for your own usage, you must legally register it. (See page 81 for more details.)

TRADE PRICE

Trade price is the wholesale price of a product, i.e., the price a licensee/ publisher/manufacturer gets for the product. This is the price on which the royalties are paid.

ROYALTIES

A royalty is a fee the licensor charges the licensee, usually a percentage of product sales.

TYPICAL ROYALTIES

Calendars	5-10%
Commercial prints	7-10%
Fabric	5-10%
Greeting cards	4-8%
Gift wrap	3-5%
Limited editions	10-15% (20% for top names)
Mugs	5%
Postcards	3-5%
Posters	7-10%
Sheets	5-8%
Shower curtains	6-8%
Stationery and gift products	4-6%
T-shirts	8-10%
Textiles	5-10%
Towels	4-8%
Various household items	4-8%
Wallpaper	5-10%
Watches	6-8%

To be successful artists must envision how their images will look on a final product.

The licensing industry is made up of several sectors.

CHARACTER AND ENTERTAINMENT

TV series – X-Files, Friends

Animated series - Tellytubbies, Rugrats, The Simpsons, South Park

Movies- Star Wars, Toy Story, Harry Potter, Lord of the Rings

Legends - Monroe, Elvis, James Dean, The Beatles

Music - Madonna, Rolling Stones, Britney Spears

SPORTS

Events - Olympics, The World Cup, Wimbledon, US Open Golf, Nascar

Individual sporting personalities - Michael Jordan, Arnold Palmer

Leagues - NFL, NHL, NFL, NBA, Major League baseball

Other - The World Wrestling Federation

FASHION

Ralph Lauren, Polo, Calvin Klein, Donna Karan

TRADEMARKS AND BRANDS

Auto industry - Jeep, Cadillac, Harley Davidson

Food – Pizza Hut, McDonalds

Drink – Coca Cola, Budweiser

CHARITY/NON PROFIT ORGANIZATIONS

National Wildlife Federation, Sierra Club

COLLEGIATE

The collegiate licensing program is a consortium of more than 60 American universities, including Georgetown, Michigan, North Carolina and Duke. This program is marketed throughout the world under a joint program as the "U.S. College Collection."

ART AND DESIGN

PROPERTY SECTORS

ART AND DESIGN SECTOR

The art and design sector is the one we will be covering in this book. It includes artists you might be familiar with: Thomas Kinkade, Christian Riese Lassen, Anne Geddes, and Mary Engelbreit, as well other less-known artists, illustrators and designers.

Within this main sector are various subdivisions. Billions of dollars' worth of product are produced and sold each year using the art and design sector. In 1999, it was estimated that 10% of the entire licensing industry came from the art and design sector. It is the fifth largest of all the sectors. The potential market is enormous. The art and design sector is less time-sensitive than the TV, movie and sports sectors. This long-term appeal transcends generations, seasons and fads. Since it is often more generic than the other categories, it has massive appeal. Included in this category is the ever-growing licensing done by museums. For museums, this is what keeps their doors open—profits from their licensing deals.

A licensee has a blank product onto which he must put a design to attract a consumer. The licensee's job is to find art that the consumer will buy. The more popular the design, the more product will be sold.

It remains for you, the artist, to create art that will sell product in sufficient quantity to give the licensee a good profit and thereby give you a reasonable return in the form of royalties.

PRODUCT CATEGORIES

Paper products – greeting cards, stationery, calendars, note cards, limited edition prints, posters, gift bags, gift boxes, bookmarks, etc.

Apparel – T-shirts, sweatshirts, children's clothing

Gift products – Cushions, stitch kits, rubber stamps, jigsaws, coasters and trays, magnets, tableware, kitchenware, porcelain products, mouse pads

Novelties – Balloons, party ware

Miscellaneous – CD inserts and cassettes, tote bags, plush toys, figurines, photograph albums, textiles, wall hangings, lamp shades, wallpaper

There are dozens of other products that are enchanced by designs and art.

Essentially, there are three types of art and design licensing:

➤ Individual

➤ Artist brand

➤ Art-as-brand

ART AND DESIGN LICENSES

INDIVIDUAL LICENSE

Every year, major publishers and manufacturers of stationery, greeting cards, jigsaws, calendars, etc. replace many of their designs to keep the range fresh and innovative. If you add up the total number of design requirements of all the greeting card companies, it is phenomenal.

An individual license is a simple license in the form of an invoice/license (see page 65) granting a licensee the rights to reproduce a single design or a small group of designs for a particular product. Because the transaction is quite small, a simple invoice can act as your full agreement with the licensee.

From a legal standpoint, it is better to have an agreement as well, which defines the terms in greater detail. Most artists usually don't have written agreements available. A licensee may provide her own agreement, which is often full of legal jargon, and on closer examination by an expert eye often reveals clauses that can be detrimental to your rights.

Some publishers, for example, put in a clause giving them the rights to sub-license your art themselves. This should be avoided at all costs. (See page 17.)

INDIVIDUAL LICENSES

A greeting card publisher sees your artwork on Christmas themes. She reviews 12 designs from your portfolio and chooses three to publish. You invoice/license her for $350—a flat fee for greeting card rights, North America only, for three years for each design (a total of $1050). These three designs will be used among some 200 card designs for the following year by the publisher.

A calendar manufacturer chooses 12 designs from your artwork to use as a calendar for a specific year (usually about two years in advance of publication). He agrees to pay you an advance of $2400 against a royalty on sales of 8%.

ARTIST BRAND LICENSE

Art brand licensing is used when an artist's name, as well as her artwork, becomes recognized.

By way of example I will give a typical scenario: A licensee loves your work so much he wants to feature you as a named artist—the product will bear your signature or perhaps your name as a logo. He wants an exclusive agreement for greeting cards, address books, journals and perhaps a few more products. His investment in turning your work into product is substantial. He will want you to sign a three- or even five-year contract term. A typical advance would be $5,000 against a minimum guaranteed payment of $10,000 for the first year. Years two, three, four and five could be $25,000 minimum guarantee, or more, if the projected sales justify it.

Recent successes are artists such as Mary Engelbreit, Christian Riese Lassen, Thomas Kinkade, and Anne Geddes.

Anne Geddes has consistently produced innovative photographs. She now has one of the most successful photographic licensing programs in the world. In this type of license, the art style is the main feature, but the artist's name also becomes recognized.

ART-AS-BRAND LICENSE

Art-as-brand is closely associated with artist brand license, except that it's not the artist and her work, but the artwork itself that becomes the brand. A classic example is "Forever Friends," which became one of the major phenomena of the 90s in the UK. Andrew Brownsword is now one of the richest men in Great Britain, all from a few drawings of cuddly teddy bears. He was absolutely brilliant in building a teddy bear concept into one of the major brands in the greeting card business, with a turnover of tens of millions. He created a range of gift ware, plush toys, mugs, pencils, pencil sharpeners, stationery, Valentine gifts and Christmas gifts—produced by the thousands. It has been one of the most successful art-as-brand licenses of the last 20 years.

In both of the licenses above, it is essential to have a detailed contract for the transaction as there are many legal implications. This is where you need the services of an intellectual property lawyer to make sure the agreement is a good one. The alternative is to have an agent negotiate the deal for you.

In the mid-80s, I art-directed a series of photographs using young children in 50s-style clothing. We did the photo shoot at an old railway station in the heart of Yorkshire, UK, which was used in the film *Fairies*. We produced a group of six images and then sold them to a major European publisher of prints, calendars, posters, postcards and greeting cards. We also sold them as T-shirts, jigsaws and a few other products. I showed the range to our Japanese agent, and similar products were licensed in Japan for many years. Over $75,000 in royalties came from just six designs, proving that the right style of work can produce great results.

WEB SITES

By spending some time on the Internet, you can study how other successful artists operate their business. They all share information about their careers and the licensing industry.

www.maryengelbreit.com
Download "Getting Started" from this site (click on "for Artists" at the bottom of the main page).

www.tracyporter.com
Some great tips on the licensing business, as well as links to many resources.

www.thomaskinkade.com

www.lassenart.com
Christian Riese Lassen's site gives you one of the greatest opportunities of seeing just what can be achieved with a licensing program.

www.swirlygirl.com
Shows the artwork of Christina Miller, an artist who is just beginning to become successful. Her site contains some very practical information about the licensing industry.

www.kathydavis.com/whatsnew/opportunities.asp
Has a frequently asked questions (FAQ) section

www.compsark.com

www.annegeddes.com

THREE SUCCESS STORIES

CHRISTIAN RIESE LASSEN

Lassen is a successful artist who runs his own licensing company from Honolulu. He has a small, dedicated team of licensing professionals who work on new licensing deals around the globe. Presently he has 70 licenses producing 400 products. These products generate around $100 million in retail sales annually. The product range includes: music boxes, checkbook covers, stained glass windows, beach towels, surf boards, T-shirts, figurines, collector plates, Lassen Hawaiian House wares, spring water, and more. His company also owns galleries in Hawaii and Las Vegas, as well as "licensed" galleries (similar to a franchise) in California, Texas, Washington, Arizona and New York. This is an example of what can be done with a unique style of artwork.

THOMAS KINKADE

Media Arts in San Diego runs a huge corporation around the work of Kinkade, who is known as "The Painter of Light." Kinkade's work consists mainly of idyllic cottages, streams, lakes and "chocolate box" landscapes, which are well-painted but a little sugary for some people. Not that that worries Mr. Kinkade: In 1999, the company's turnover was over $100 million from a huge merchandising campaign in the American market. In terms of merchandise sold, he may be the world's most popular artist.

MARY ENGELBREIT

Engelbreit was successful in the 90s with a number of designs appearing on greeting cards, calendars, stationery, table mats, and more. She even has her own magazine, *Home Companion*, since 1996 as well as her own store in her hometown of St Louis, Missouri. Mary's work is licensed to more than 40 manufacturers with more than 6500 products. She has a deal to illustrate 20 children's books over the next few years.

Define your style of artwork: _____

_____

_____

What particular theme do you work in? _____

_____

Are any of these styles commercial? ❑ Yes ❑ No

If no, how can you make them more commercial? _____

_____

_____

_____

What products would your work look best on? _____

_____

_____

_____

Have you researched this product in stores and magazines?

What magazines have you read to familiarize yourself with
licensing? _____

_____

_____

How many pieces of artwork do you have available for licensing?

_____

ACTION PLAN

Use the answers to the
questions at left to create
your action plan.

1.
_____

2.
_____

3.
_____

4.
_____

5.
_____

6.
_____

7.
_____

8.
_____

9.
_____

10.
_____

Chapter 2
Marketplaces

Art does not reproduce the visible, rather, it makes visible.

Paul Klee

PRODUCT CATEGORIES

While this is not a full list, it will give you an idea of the broad range of products on which licensees pay royalties. It will also give you an indication of why the market is so vast and how much scope there is.

PRODUCTS

Address books	Baby wear	Balloons
Bath accessories	Bedding	Books
Bookmarks	Calendars	Cassette covers
CD inserts	Children's books	Christmas cards
Clocks	Clothing	Coffee mugs
Collector plates	Confectionery	Diaries
Dinnerware	Figurines	Frames
Framed prints	Gift bags	Gift boxes
Gift wrap	Gift ware	Greeting cards
Jewelry	Jigsaw puzzles	Journals
Key ring	Kitchen textiles	Lamp shades
Limited editions	Linens	Luggage
Magnets	Melamine mugs	Musical boxes
Needlework kits	Paper tableware	Party note cards
Pencils	Pet products	Phone cards
Photograph albums	Pillows	Place mats
Plaques	Plates	Playing cards
Porcelain table top	Postcards	Posters
Pottery	Prints	Rugs
Scarves	Screen savers	Stamps
Stationery	Stickers	Sweatshirts
T-Shirts	Tableware	Table mats
Tea	Textiles	Ties
Tiles	Tinware	Toiletries
Towels	Toys	Trading cards
Transfers	Trays	Trinket boxes
Valentine gift lines	Wall decor	Wall hangings

Adapt a long-term outlook for your licensing career.

GREETING CARDS

The greeting card industry is a multi-billion-dollar industry, with such companies as Hallmark, American Greetings, Recycled Paper Products, CR Gibson and Interart dominating the business. There are many other medium-sized companies such as Design Design, Marian Heath Greetings, Red Farm Studios, Leanin' Tree and Marcel Schurman that are very successful. There are also many smaller companies specializing in a particular style, some of which are owner/artist-run or small partnerships.

Greeting cards can be a good starting point for artists beginning to license their art. It is a good bread-and-butter category, one which should not be ignored. Some publishers even put a small bio on the back of each card—great PR for any artist. You will also be able to buy cards at wholesale and use them as publicity material.

One of the most important facts about becoming a good greeting card artist is understanding how cards are sold. This may seem obvious, but it is often overlooked. Cards normally appear in racks, particularly in the big stores or specialty card shops. The top third of the card is what the customer sees. Out of the hundreds and hundreds of designs available, does the top third of the card you've designed give the buyer a good idea of what the card's sentiment is, or the occasion?

What makes a person pick a particular card? Go out and buy a card for an imaginary occasion. See how you respond to certain designs. Why did you choose the one you did? Designers need to consider who the buyer of the card will be and what occasion the card is for, as well as the age group.

Get to know each greeting card publisher's range before you submit work. In some cases, they will have criteria that have to be adhered to: preferred paper stock, sizes, proportions, subject matter, color, media.

Large corporations such as Hallmark and American Greetings design much of their work in-house, but they do have openings for freelance contributors. Their standards are high, and you must understand the greeting card market to stand any chance of success with them. While much of this work is pure greeting-card material, i.e., general birthdays, congratulations, birth of your baby, anniversary, wedding, get well, etc., fine art is still used in many ranges. These companies are especially interested in a particular style of art that fits into a range they already produce.

Over 2.6 billion Christmas cards are sent anually in the United States. Hallmark alone has over 2300 designs. Over 80 million graduation cards were sold in 1996.

29

SUBMISSIONS

To submit to a publisher, you will need to prepare at least six to twelve examples. If you send 24 designs and they like the overall style, they may choose six or twelve to publish.

Style is very important to greeting card publishers, and they are on the lookout for artists who have an original way of looking at subjects that have been done a thousand times previously. In some ways, nothing appears to be original in the card market, but the way the work is executed can give a worn-out theme a fresh, new look.

The small, specialized greeting card companies produce beautiful cards. Invariably the print runs are quite small initially. They don't have the budgets of the large multinationals. These companies can, however, be a good starting point, particularly if your work fits into their niche market. Royalties are generally lower than with the large companies.

CARD MOCK-UPS

These days it's very easy to do laser mock-ups of cards on your own color printer. This is by far the best type of presentation to a greeting-card publisher. It will also help you see what a group of cards looks like together. Look at the colors. When they're all laid out together, is there enough contrast in the range? What is showing in the top third of the card?

FORMAT

➤ Size is not so relevant; proportions are. Since most cards are 5x7", you can't go wrong if your art is created in this size, or a proportionate size.

➤ Only 5–10% of cards created fall into unusual formats. While there are possibilities in this slightly more niche market, many publishers won't print anything other than standard-size cards.

ROYALTIES

Greeting card royalties vary from around 4 - 8% .

RESOURCE

The Greeting Card Association
1156 15th St NW #900, Washington, DC 20005
202·393·1778
www.greetingcard.org
The information available through this association is invaluable.

TRADE SHOW

National Stationery Show
George Little Management
800·222·SHOW
www.glmshows.com   <info@glmshows.com>
Held in mid-May in New York City. A major event covering gifts, stationery, greeting cards and many other products.

ATTENDING THE NATIONAL STATIONERY SHOW

➤ Educate yourself several months in advance of attending on the greeting card industry. Browse stores and specialty shops. What style of artwork is being printed on cards these days?

➤ If you find a card that has artwork close to your style, write down the publisher's name for your in-house mailing list, as well as to check out when you arrive at the show.

➤ Have an aim, i.e., are you looking for an agent, publishers of greeting cards, just getting an introduction to the business?

➤ Exhibitors seem to welcome artists and their portfolios at this show—it's actually part of the show agenda—so bring an easy-to-view, small portfolio; no slides.

➤ Bring plenty of business cards, post cards, photos or anything that you can leave with a potential publisher.

➤ Take a taxi right to the door of the Jacob Javitts Convention Center in Manhattan. Save your energy for the show. If you are staying at one of the hotels cooperating with this event (listed in the information you receive from the promoters), you can take a jitney bus to the show for free. They go to and fro all day. Even if you are not staying at the hotel, you can catch the bus for free if you know which hotels have stops.

➤ Order your entry pass to the show ahead of time. It will save time and last-minute hassles.

➤ Scan the aisles, looking for your style of artwork. The show can be overwhelming. It's huge and has hundreds of exhibitors.

➤ Walk down the center of the aisles so everyone doesn't stop you.

➤ Stop at a booth where you feel the art style fits yours or if there is a sign saying "Artists Welcome."

➤ Dress in layers—the Javitts Center is kept very cold.

➤ Some people take a small suitcase on rollers to carry all the materials they gathered.

➤ Write notes on the backs of the business cards you collect—key words that will jog your memory—"*Send photos of landscapes by July to Jan Williams.*"

➤ Do not be afraid to ask questions. Make a list of questions you may want to ask about working with a publisher before arriving at the show.

➤ Besides greeting card companies, you will find stationery companies and other potential licensees interested in images for a variety of products.

PRINTS

As in all markets, published want professionalism, reliability and a regular supply of work to review from their artists. A print publisher is trying to create a print with a strong theme or identity. Success in the print market depends on whether you are with a publisher who has good distribution.

There are several subcategories in the print marketplace:

➤ Mass-market posters and prints

➤ High-end prints

➤ Limited-edition lithos

➤ Silk screens

➤ Giclées

A lithograph (otherwise known as a litho) uses a four- to six-color process on an offset litho printer, making a reproduction of an image from four basic colors of ink: yellow, magenta, cyan and black. An extra color or two can be printed to enhance the reproduction quality. Color separations are made from a transparency of the original artwork using halftone screens and filters to separate each color (a printing plate can be made for each color). When paper is passed through the machine, it basically prints one color on top of the other to create a reproduction of the image. If you look at the printed image under a magnifying glass, you can see dots. Much of the printed imagery available is created using this process, i.e., greeting cards, calendars, posters, stationery, etc.

The next three categories are printed using this process.

The print market can help an artist to become well known, not only in the US but in Europe as well.

MASS-MARKET POSTERS AND PRINTS

Sometimes referred to as mass-produced lithos, these prints sell at low prices to frame shops, department stores, chain stores, gift shops, home furnishing stores, boutiques, and even swap meets and flea markets. You may have worked at an office where salesmen have sold them door-to-door. Retail prices range from $5 - 50, often including frame. In most cases, the frame costs far more than the print. The print can cost the retailer as little as 25¢.

This market is difficult for fine artists, as publishers try to license work very inexpensively, sometimes offering flat fees only. Quite often, publishers have to sell a vast amount of prints for an artist to see any substantial amounts of money if a royalty deal is agreed upon.

Photographing a painting that has a great deal of texture can be difficult, thus making it hard to get a good quality print. Light catching the texture causes a 'flair.'

To ensure that you are getting a decent deal with the publisher, you need to inquire what his selling prices are and what quantities he sells. The trade price given may be $3.00, but what discount does he give for large orders? The actual selling price could be as low as 25¢. For instance: the publisher makes a large sale of 5000 prints. The purchaser, a framer, pays only 25¢ per print. He then frames the print and sells it in quantity to a retail store for $15.00. The print itself makes up very little of the cost. Since the artist is paid by the publisher on the publisher's selling price, the artist receives only 10% of 5000 x 25¢, or a total of $125.

If the artwork was licensed to a higher-end print publisher who only sold 2500 copies of the print at $4.00, at 10% that would be $1000 for the artist—a huge difference in royalties.

This market can be quite lucrative if you choose a publisher carefully and you are on a royalty arrangement. My first deal in this market, nearly 20 years ago, emphasizes this point. I sold the rights to a series of images, which were quite different from anything else on the market at the time. The publisher refused to pay a royalty as he felt he was taking a big risk. I ended up doing a deal for around $300 per image (for world print rights). They sold tens of thousands and had a massive success, and my company and the artist didn't receive one additional cent over the initial $300. Had we had a royalty arrangement, we would have earned thousands of dollars. It is therefore important always to require a royalty. The only alternative to a royalty, if the publisher refuses and you still want to do a deal, is to insist on a fixed-quantity print run. That way, if he wants to print more, he has to come back to you and pay you again for each new print run.

Ask for an advance against a royalty (of 7-10%) of $200 - 500.

HIGH-END PRINTS

High-end prints are better-quality lithographic reproduction prints and posters, printed on better-quality paper, reserved for better-quality art with unlimited print runs. These can be sold (framed or unframed) in department stores such as Nieman Marcus and Macy's, higher-end frame and gallery shops, as well as home furnishing stores. Styles vary enormously. There are dozens and dozens of publishers in this marketplace. It is still regarded as a mass-market product, but the emphasis is on a much higher quality of product. They are often framed nicely with unusual mats, adding value to the product.

LIMITED-EDITION LITHOS

Limited-edition lithos vary in edition size but usually range from 50–950 copies. Retail prices vary from around $20 for small prints to as much as $750, and even more for well-known artists. The average price, however, is $75 - 250, depending on the dimensional size and quantity of prints in the edition.

As in other print markets, publishers are looking for a consistent quality of art from an artist. They require a steady flow of work to choose from. The investment is high for publishers in this category, so they must choose reliable artists who understand and accept the long-term implications of producing limited editions. It often means this type of contract comes after you have "put your time in the industry"—after you have a reputation.

In this market, the publisher will usually produce glossy catalogs, instigate PR and advertise extensively—always with a view to a long-term investment. Artists such as Robert Bateman, John Seerey-Lester, Carl Brenders, Douglas Hoffman, Heindel and Simon Bull have created a great collectors' market via their respective publishers.

You will need to provide an extensive body of work, not just 10-12 pieces. Publishers like to see at least 20 pieces, so they can assess the consistency of quality and style before accepting an artist to publish. Initially, select five to six of your best pieces to submit. You will then have more to show at a later date if requested.

Limited-edition contracts are usually royalty-based as well as exclusive. Many publishers promote the artist quite heavily by producing special advertising campaigns and brochures. Promotion like this really helps to build the artist's profile and reputation. This in turn can lead to higher prices for originals. No publisher wants to promote an artist and spend huge amounts on PR only to have the artist work with other publishers who are competitors.

The only problem an artist might encounter is how to protect herself if the publisher doesn't push the work enough—if he backs off a particular edition—leaving you tied to an exclusive deal with no income.

Many publishers have websites. Spend some time researching. An investment of time here will pay off in the future.

www.millpond.com
www.greenwichworkshop.com
www.artinmotion.com
www.galaxyofgraphics.com
www.bonnart.com
www.wildapple.com
www.bmcgaw.com
www.graphiquedefrance.com
www.portalpublications.
www.michaelsfineart.com
www.artimpressionsgallery.com

CONSIDERATIONS

➤ One good way to protect yourself is to ask if the publisher can publish a series—at least four to six per year.

➤ Limit the contract to three years, with an option to renew at the end of three years. This way you don't tie yourself for a long period with a publisher who isn't doing well for you.

➤ After the second year, have a minimum-income figure written into the contract. After the first year, you can terminate if the income drops below a certain amount.

➤ You need to be flexible if this is your first publishing agreement. It is important to have an "out" if things go wrong. Exclusive contracts are quite often necessary, but the publisher must allow you some protection if things don't work out.

SILK SCREENS

These days, silk screens are usually produced from transparencies of the art, which are then scanned. Silk screens are produced with an average of 15 colors—up to as many as 100 colors for special works of art. The edition quantity can vary enormously, from 15-295 but can be more.

POTENTIAL INCOME

Some publishers may pay you up front for an edition; however the royalty rate may then be less. In the following example, you might earn $2000. Depending on your cashflow, this could actually be quite a good deal, as you are guaranteed this amount even if the edition doesn't sell out.

295 (edition size) x $90 average sales price (allowing for discounts) = $26,550

Royalty rate of 10% = $2655 royalty for artist

GICLÉES

Giclée printing is a relatively new process for the art world. While it's been around for almost 10 years, it's only recently become widely accepted. Giclée comes from the French word for "splatter," which is more or less how the ink is applied to the paper. The Iris printer was the first machine to produce this type of print. In the early days, many people had reservations about the longevity of the prints, mostly due to the quality of the ink. In recent years, better inks and papers have been developed. Many firms in the US and Europe offer high-quality prints. The beauty of the giclée process is that you can print one at a time, thereby reducing upfront output of money drastically.

Quite a number of publishers are now selling giclées. They are regarded by many to be as good as a silk screen. There are, however, an equal number of publishers who are still suspicious of this process—they continue to regard giclées with contempt. Giclées are gradually changing the whole picture of the publishing industry, as they allow individual artists to publish limited editions at extremely low costs, empowering themselves as self-published artists. (Read more in Chapter 7.)

To produce a typical medium-sized print can cost as little as $50 (the initial setup and scanning charges are normally around $100). It is possible to get smaller prints done for as little as $25.

There's more about giclées in Chapter 6.

SELL YOUR ART OVER AND OVER AND OVER AGAIN

by Michael Gordon

As a fine-art printer, I have often been asked, "Which painting should I print?" Having been in hundreds of artists' studios over the years, I have made a single observation that has aided in answering this question. Mixed in with all the artwork hanging on the wall is one special gem. Its price tag is marked **NFS** (not for sale). This piece is generally the artist's latest and favorite creation—one she is still emotionally attached to. This is the one that should be made into a giclée edition. The artist can then enjoy the financial benefits of that artwork without selling the original.

At Triumphant Printing, we print limited-edition giclées for a wide range of artists—from the newly graduated student to the mid-career artist to the well-established and highly collected artist. Giclée limited editions have provided each of these artists with additional exposure in the marketplace, as well as increased income. For example, there are artists for whom we print whose originals sell in the $100,000+ range. Collectors of these artists' work can now collect more pieces in the form of giclées, which sell for only a fraction of the original.

An art enthusiast who currently doesn't have the pocketbook to purchase the original is able to start collecting an artist's work through the purchase of giclées. He will often continue to buy prints and, hopefully, may aspire one day to purchase an original.

In editioning a print, the giclée process can provide artists with the benefit of not having to print the full edition all at once. They may choose to print an edition of 75, but only print the first 20 initially. Having a small up-front cost has allowed an artist to finance the balance of the edition through the sales of the initial print run. There are countless stories of artists and publishers who have gone the route of offset lithography, only to end up with boxes and boxes of prints. The same budget can now be used to launch multiple, small, limited editions, thus allowing buyers the choice of a variety of images.

Recently, a major art publication showed the results of a current survey. It noted giclées as the leading type of print that galleries have added to their mix of art offerings. Giclée prints ranked in sales above serigraphs, etchings, engravings and woodcuts. Giclées sit firmly in third place, surpassed only by posters and lithographs. I can think of no other printing style that has shown up in galleries and museums around the world with as strong an acceptance as giclée.

Michael Gordon is a printer and colorist at Triumphant Printers, a printer of giclées produced for galleries in Europe, the United Kingdom and throughout North America. Triumphant Printers is located at 11 Watkins Ave, Oneonta, NY 13820 607/433-2644. www.studiogiclee.com <vze2n29@verizon.net>

CALENDARS

Calendars are a multi-billion-dollar industry. They come in many sizes and shapes. Some popular calendars from previous years were inspirational or humorous: Ansel Adams; Magic Eyes; Sierra Wilderness; cats; Mary Engelbreit; angels; Anne Geddes; Dilbert: Ask Me How My Day Went; Disney Days; Far Side Desk Calendar; Friends; Georgia O'Keeffe; Goosebumps; Life's Little Instruction Calendar; The Muppets; Rottweilers; Winnie-the-Pooh.

If you have an idea for a 2005 calendar, contact the publishers no later than the early fall of 2003. Prepare a letter that describes your calendar concept and includes final art reproductions of exactly how the calendar will look. With such great computer output these days, this is no longer a difficult task. Send your query to several publishers at once. If you don't hear back from them within 45 days, make a follow-up call.

Usually, calendar publishers are looking for a concept (as well as quality in execution). A hot idea will get you in the door fast.

Most publishers have specific policies regarding the sale and distribution of calendars to retailers, and the discounts they expect to receive. Negotiating terms as an artist will be difficult. You most likely will have to go with their terms with respect to advances but you should be able to command a royalty of 5 - 10%.

RESOURCES

Calendar Market Association
Dick Mikes
710 E Ogden Ave, Naperville, IL 60563
630/579-3264   630/369-2488 Fax
www.calendarmarketplace.com <cma@b-online.com>
They publish a book called Publishing and Marketing Your Calendar.

Calendar Advertising Council
PO Box 15092, Austin, TX 78761
512/323-0735
www.ppai.org

Publishers Weekly
800/662-4445
In March each year they publish a calendar issue. Buy it to find out what the big publishers are doing. $6.50

You can also rent a list of calendar publishers' names and addresses for one-time use on pressure-sensitive labels. 175 publishers/$44ppd. Call 800/ 383-0677.

COLLECTOR PLATES

While the multi-million-dollar plate market has had a hard time recently, it is still a very lucrative market. Companies such as Franklin Mint and Bradford Exchange are the major players. These companies usually build an artist-as-brand concept by utilizing the artwork of a particular artist to create a series of collector plates.

Approaching these companies is not difficult. Coming up with a quality concept, however, which will sell and stand out from the crowd is becoming more and more difficult. These companies spend a small fortune in advertising in the color supplements to the Sunday newspaper magazine.

Royalties vary from 1-5%. With the massive quantities they sell, these low royalties can still bring in large sums. Advances can be quite reasonable, from $500-2000 per design, and more if you get a reputation in this market.

This area should only be tackled when you have confidence in your art and you are producing work of a high standard. Each series of plates needs to have a theme or story so that they can be marketed as a set.

The age range of the buyers is usually 35 – 65 (the average age being 50) and most are female. Keep this in mind from the outset. Does your work appeal to that market?

Study the market carefully before approaching these companies. It's best to have a track record and some recognition (but not always necessary). This helps with the hype attached to the marketing side of this product category. Most of the hype is just that—hype: "One of the world's best wildlife artists." Basically, you can say that about anyone who is talented! So don't believe all the hype. If you are producing the "perfect style of artwork" that they believe will sell, then they will be interested.

MAJOR COMPANIES

See the listings in Chapter 10 for:

➤ Bradford Exchange

➤ Franklin Mint

➤ Hamilton Collection Inc

➤ Reco International Corp

There are many product categories you can consider. Don't be too ambitious at first. Look carefully at what you do, and relate your work to particular products that will fit your style well. Choose half a dozen companies in each category and target your work carefully.

JIGSAW PUZZLES

There are quite a number of manufacturers in this category. Each year, these companies replace a good number of designs. Do your homework at the National Stationery Show or at your local retail stores to see what subject matter they like.

Jigsaws need to have visual interest throughout the entire layout of the work. Avoid submitting work with large areas of plain sky or sidewalk. Twenty pieces of plain blue sky could make a jigsaw addict quite irritated!

RESOURCES

Great American Puzzle Factory
Patricia Duncan
16 S Main St, Norwalk, CT 06854-2981
203/838-2065
www. greatamericanpuzzle.com   <ashevlin@greatamericanpuzzle.com>

Ceaco
Lisa Casella
124 Watertown St, Watertown, MA 02172
617/926-8080   617/924-7554 Fax
www.ceaco-inc.com

Hasbro
www.hasbro.com

Ravensburger
www.ravensburger.de

www.americanpuzzles.com
For a list of manufacturers

MISCELLANEOUS MARKETS

Listen to the market. If you give it what it wants, you will be successful.

TABLE MATS, TRAYS, COASTERS

These companies buy new designs quite regularly. Fees are reasonable. Trade shows are the best way to see who is out there and what they produce. Also visit stores that stock these products.

NEEDLECRAFT AND STITCH KITS

This market is dominated by a small number of manufacturers. Designs are generally converted by computer these days. Not a big money earner, but a possible source of extra income.

RESOURCE

Dimensions
Pamela Keller
1801 N 12th St, Reading, PA 19604
610/939-9900 610/939-9666 Fax
www.dimensions-crafts.com   <pam.keller@dimensions-crafts.com>
A needlecraft manufacturer. Their products are sold in catalogs and craft chains. They work with over 100 artists and review work year-round. They are actively seeking new artists. Submit a portfolio (they prefer color copies, brochure) for review by mail or e-mail.

STATIONERY AND GIFT PRODUCTS

Most department stores such as J C Penney, Target, Macy's, as well as chains such as Papyrus, Hallmark Stores, Borders, Barnes & Noble, and good gift shops, carry a range of stationery, back-to-school items and gift ware—mugs, photo albums, calendars, notelets, etc. These product categories offer artists other sources of revenue for their designs.

RESOURCES

Dayspring
PO Box 1010, Siloam Springs, AR 72761-1010

Portal Publications
201 Alameda del Prado #200, Novato, CA 94949-6657
Greeting-card and print publisher

Study the many magazines listed in the back of this book to discover more aspects of the industry.

Paper Adventures
Shanna de la Cruz
901 S 5th St, Milwaukee, WI 53204
414/383-0414 ext 255 414/645-0760 Fax
www.paperadventures.com <shanna.dc@paperadventures.com>
Their products go in craft and notecard stores. They print invitations in a variety of styles. You can e-mail your samples (as a jpg), send a CD or send non-returnable samples in the mail. They like to see your progress with quarterly postcards of new works.

TABLEWARE

This market of mugs, plates, bowls, etc. is notoriously difficult. Many of the manufacturers in this industry produce a lot of their design work in-house. In the last few years, some companies have bought outside designs. This industry is far behind the times in some ways, as is reflected in their fee schedules. It is getting better, however. There are a number of innovative companies who make some good artistic products.

WALLCOVERING COMPANIES

There are many companies that supply decorative wallpapers for the retail markets.

RESOURCES

Eisenhart Wallcoverings Co
Steven Mellott
1649 Broadway, Hanover, PA 17331
717/632-8024
www.eisenwalls.com <smellott@eisenhart.net>

Imperial Wallcoverings
Lori Russell
23645 Mercantile Rd, Cleveland, OH 44094
216/2765-8763 216/292-3206

EXAMPLE

You license your concept for a range of children's T-shirts, to be sold in Target and other retail stores. It's September and the product is for spring of the following year. Trade price for the T-shirt is $6. Initial print run is 5000; four designs (total of 20,000 T-shirts).

$6 x 20,000	$120,000
Royalty @ 6%	$7200
Advance	$3000
Guarantee	$7000

Guarantee is for the period September - December 31 of the following year (16 months later) and a further guarantee of $7000 for the second full year.

During the year you will receive a royalty report each quarter. Probably for the first two quarters, your royalties will show a negative balance (due to your advance). Once sales have exceeded a certain amount and the royalties earned reach $3000, then you will start to receive a quarterly royalty check. At the end of the year, if there is a shortfall, then the manufacturer will have to pay you the difference between the royalties you've received and the guaranteed amount.

BOOKS

Many artists' work could be used as cover designs for books. Several fine artists have taken advantage of this venue. Most publishers use the exact artwork for their book cover design. If the cover is a success they will want to use another piece, perhaps even commission a special piece. Usually, you create the piece in whatever size you normally do (but preferably in proportion to the size of the book); then the book publisher sends a photographer to photograph it meticulously for reproduction. The exposure your distinct style can receive on a bestselling book cover is phenomenal.

SUCCESS STORY

One artist's first book-cover commission was a bestseller. She became almost as well known as the author! Soon she had 20 book covers under her wings, as well as several children's books, some which she illustrated and others which she both illustrated and wrote. This brought her recognition in other venues as well.

LOCATING BOOK PUBLISHERS

➤ Browse through bookstores. Publishers list their data near the front of most books.

➤ Attend the annual trade show, Book Expo.

➤ Mail samples of your work to book publishers (see Chapter 10) to introduce them to your style of artwork.

➤ *Literary Market Place* lists publishers and the types of books they publish.

CHILDREN'S BOOKS

The children's book market is a very specialized field. Most projects pay little compared to other industries. A typical 32-page book could take you 8 - 12 weeks to complete, from art roughs to finished art. You need to gauge the fee paid to the time involved, as well as your talent and love for this venue.

If you have your own ideas for children's books:

➤ Figure out your age group

➤ Find out the typical page count a publisher prints

➤ Design a layout

➤ Produce a cover

➤ Mock up two to three pages, with the rest of the book as pencil sketches. Using a computer, lay out the book as you think it might look. This will help you pace the words with the illustrations (often overlooked).

ROYALTIES

➤ Often a flat fee when doing a cover or illustration

➤ A 10% royalty is usually agreed, but this would be split if there were a writer and an illustrator. Book contracts will also include various royalty rates for overseas sales, book clubs and special editions.

➤ Advances against royalties are often given.

CHILDREN'S BOOK AGENT

Kendra Marcus
67 Meadow View Rd, Orinda, CA 94563-3246
925/254-2664
www.bookstoliteracy.com

Contact over 400 book publishers via direct mail. $40 for list on pressure-sensitive mailing labels from ArtNetwork at 800·383·0677.

TRADE SHOWS

Book Expo

383 Main Ave, Norwalk, CT 06051

800/840-5614   203/840-5614

www.bookexpoamerica.com <inquiry@bookexpoamerica.com>
Beginning of May in New York

The Bologna Book Fair

Piazza Costituzine 6, 40128 Bologna Italy

www.bolognafiere.it <bookfaire@bolognafiere.it>
This trade show has a section for individual artists to show their work, as well as a publication and special exhibition, which also travels to Japan. They have an illustrators' "cafe" where various events take place, one being meetings with the jury of the exhibition to discuss reasons for their selections.

RESOURCES

Publishers Weekly

245 W 17th St, New York, NY 10011

212/463-6758
Take a look at what designs are on the new book covers

How

800/289-0963
This magazine has articles on book illustration and design.

Art for the Written Word

by Wendell Minor and Florence Friedman Minor

Jackets Required: An illustrated History of American Book Jacket Design

by Steven Heller and Seymour Chast

Covers & Jackets! What the Best-Dressed Books & Magazines Are Wearing

by Steven Heller and Anne Fink

Children's Writer's & Illustrator's Market

Writer's Digest Books

800/289-0963

ANIMATION

Revenues can be huge if the animated series is a success.

Ideas for an animated TV series can come from a variety of sources—books, comic strips, as well as ideas developed specifically for the market. Picture storybooks, such as Peter Rabbit, were such a success that licenses were sold to manufacturers to produce baby's and children's products, selling to an entire generation of mothers who read the stories to their children and who in many cases had actually read them as children themselves. Cartoon strips like Peanuts, Dennis the Menace and Garfield eventually became animated series. In the above cases, major merchandise programs were created, generating millions of dollars' worth of merchandise.

TV series featuring Arthur, Barney and many, many more were also created from an idea for a character who captured the imagination, who in turn was gradually turned into a successful property through determination and good marketing.

Creating a property for animation is a long, arduous process, sometimes taking as many as seven years to broadcast! There are no simple, set rules in this industry, and no two deals are the same.

An original animated series generally begins by taking the form of a style guide and synopsis, together with character studies of each character, as well as various story outlines for the series. It also includes background scenes and images which show how the characters relate to each other or their environment. Most animation series are 13, 26 or 52 episodes; the episode length can be approximately 5, 15 or 30 minutes, although the actual running time is less due to advertisements. A quarter-hour episode is usually 13 minutes long.

The more detailed the style guide, the better the chances of attracting interest. Interest can come from animation production studios, broadcasters, agents and investors. Quite often, it can be a combination of several parties.

Creating a pilot can cost anything from a few thousand dollars to $100,000 and more. Once a pilot is made, it doesn't necessarily mean the series will be created. At this stage, the idea has to be sold to broadcasters in order to finance the $4 million it will probably cost to make an initial series. Getting a new series onto the screen is a complex process that can take many years.

If the project has merchandise possibilities, then several months or a year ahead of broadcast, license deals are negotiated for toys, games and a host of merchandise.

Quite often, creators have to assign their rights to a production company or development company, as many of these companies will not invest the large amounts of money required unless they have complete control. If this is the case, you need a good lawyer who is in the entertainment business to help you in the negotiations.

RESOURCES

Animation World Network

6525 Sunset Blvd #8, Hollywood, CA 90028

323/606-4200

www.awn.com   <info@awn.com>

They publish a magazine, have career connections, discussion forums, school directory and more.

International Animation Association/ASIFA

www.swcp.com/~asifa

KIDS MAGAZINES

Kidscreen

www.kidscreen.com

Animation Magazine

www.animationmagazine.net

STAMPS

by Constance Smith

Each year the US Postal Service receives over 40,000 consumer requests for new subjects to appear on postage stamps. From those requested, approximately 30 subjects are chosen, utilizing an average of 100 designs. (One subject matter may be depicted on several stamps.) The final selection of subjects is made by the Citizens' Stamp Advisory Committee/ CSAC. Subjects are selected three years in advance of issuance.

The total commission for a completed stamp design or illustration is $3000. The artist is given $1000 upon signing an agreement for concepts. If the work is approved, the artist receives an additional $2000 for the final art.

When approved, the subjects are assigned to the Postal Service Stamp Design staff. The design staff works with five highly qualified, professional art directors in developing the designs.

The US Postal Service continually searches for new and creative talent to utilize in its design program. New artists are commissioned each year. Creating stamp designs is not an easy task. It requires unique talent, style and discipline to work within the parameters required to create art to be reproduced on such a small scale.

The US Postal Service does not grant interviews. If you think you meet the requirements as a professional designer, illustrator or photographer and wish to be considered for a stamp design assignment, the guidelines are as follows:

➤ All work must be submitted in print form (tear sheets, color copies, etc.) that will be retained by the US Postal Service. They will be made available to art directors in the event a work is approved. Original art or slides will not be accepted.

The US Postal Service will contact you if they are interested in commissioning your service. The US Postal Service will not:

➤ Acknowledge receipt of samples by letter or phone

➤ Offer reasons for rejection of submission

This case is the only exception to the rule of not relinquishing your copyright!

➤ The USPS insists on retaining the copyright on all images they use, as well as ownership of the original artwork, which is often deposited either in the Postal Museum or the Smithsonian Institute.

➤ If a stamp is popular, the artist may be asked to sign uncut sheets, which could mean $1-4 per signature depending on the sheet and edition.

SUCCESS STORY

Remember the artist who had her artwork on the cover of a best-selling novel? Well, her artwork is also on a U.S. postage stamp! The U.S. Postal Service was looking for an artist to do a Kwanza stamp. Through detective work and a little help from the Internet, they landed at her site.

Though she receives no further royalties for her image (which has been used for over three years now) she sure gets a lot of image PR! Millions of people have seen her artwork over and over again. Though the post office owns the original (and the copyright), she is able to make similar pieces into posters, cards and book covers!

RESOURCE

US Postal Service Citizens' Stamp Advisory Committee/CSAC

475 L'Enfant Plaza SW, Room 4474E, Washington, DC 20260-2437

202/268-2000

www.usps.gov

Ask for a guideline on becoming a designer. Designs for U.S. postage stamps are reviewed and accepted by a committee of 11 people, 18 months in advance of the publication date.

UNITED NATIONS

The United Nations Postal Administration/UNPA also runs a stamp program. Fees average $2000 for one image, or if multiple images are used, $1000 per image (maximum fee for a series is $12,000). The UN retains the copyright, but the artist retains the artwork. They try to maintain a global perspective and thus are looking for work from international artists.

RESOURCE

UNPA

Robert Stein

2 UN Plaza, DC 2-622, New York, NY 10017

212/963-4329

Send non-returnable samples (color photocopies or slides) for review. They publish seven stamps per year. In 2002 they were working with Peter Max.

FOREIGN STAMPS

Inter-Governmental Philatelic Corporation is an agent to foreign governments. They produce postage stamps and related items on behalf of 40 different governments. They work with 75-100 artists each year, preferring artists within metropolitan New York or that tri-state area. Artwork must be focused, four-color and reproducible to stamp size. They prefer air brush, acrylic and gouache. If you send them a portfolio, it should contain four-color illustrations of realistic flora, fauna, technical subjects, autos or ships.

RESOURCE

Inter-Governmental Philatelic Corporation/IGPC
460 W 34th St #10Fl, New York, NY 10001
212/629-7979
www.igpc.net   <postmaster@igpc.net>
Include samples of original artwork reduced to stamp size.

WILDLIFE STAMPS

Wildlife art is big business in the US. Besides posters, there are wildlife stamps. Stamp publishing is considered prestigious in the wildlife art world. State conservation departments and organizations, as well as federal resources, sponsor contests throughout the year.

RESOURCE

Wildlife Art Magazine
1428 Cliff Rd E, Burnsville, MN 55337
www.wildlifeartmag.com
They publish a Wildlife Art Stamp Guide ($7ppd) annually in January that lists hundreds of competitions across the nation.

STOCK PHOTOGRPAHY AND ILLUSTRATION

Stock art is a $200-million-a-year market. Generally, stock images are licensed via buyers' catalogs, a directory, direct mail, CD-ROM or the Internet. The artist grants an agency the right (often exclusive) to re-license selected images of her work for specific jobs: advertising, book covers, brochures, magazines, annual reports and the like.

Artists generally show a small selection to begin with, and, if they are popular, the stock agency will contract more of their work.

Generally, the artist has to bear the full cost of transparencies and duplicates of the images used. This cost can get out of hand if your agency requests 50 trannies of all 50 of your artworks, for instance. Make it clear in the contract where your limits lie.

Stock houses have become large and impersonal corporations, seeking fees from rights to art that may not be in your best interest. An artist often does not have the right after signing with an agency to refuse usage. Sometimes an artist must grant an agency the right to alter, tint, crop or otherwise manipulate images.

Agencies in this genre of licensing are abundant. They can be found in the local *Yellow Pages* or through a directory of illustration such as *The Black Book, The Graphic Artists Guild Directory of Illustration, RSVP* or *The Workbook*.

Fees are generally received by the agency and split 50/50 with the artist.

STOCK ART

Dynamic Graphics
6000 N Forest Park Dr, Peoria, IL 61614-3592
800/255-8800   309/688-8800   309/688-5873 Fax
www.dgusa.com

Getty Images
601 N 34th St, Seattle, WA 98103
877/438-8966   206/925-5000
www.gettyone.com

Indexed Visuals
866/4-IVPICS
www.indexedvisuals.com

The Online Illustration Source
145 Cabot St #6, Beverly, MA 01915
978/921-0887
www.illo.com   <stuff@illo.com>

Stockart.com
155 N College Ave #225, Ft Collins, CO 80524
800/297-7658   970/493-0087   970/493-6997 Fax
www.stockart.com   <stockart@stockart.com>

Stock Illustration Source
16 W 19th St #9Fl, New York, NY 10011
800/4-IMAGES (446-2437)   212/849-2900   212/691-6609 Fax
www.images.com   <sis@images.com>
They work with over 1200 illustrators and artists.

NEWSLETTER

PhotoStock Notes
PhotoSource International
Ron Engh
Pine Lake Farm, 1910 35th Rd, Osceola, WI 54020-5602
715/248-3800
www.photosource.com   <info@photosource.com>
A monthly newsletter that keeps you informed about the stock photography business.

The record industry also uses fine artists for CD and cassette inserts. You could propose a particular idea for a CD cover for your favorite entertainer, or show them your style in general.

RECORD COMPANIES

Capital Records
Tommy Steele
1750 N Vine St, Hollywood, CA 90028-5274
323/462-6252
www.hollywoodandvine.com

Virgin Records
Steve Gerdes
338 N Foothill Rd, Beverly Hills, CA 90210
310/278-1181   310/288-1490 Fax

RESOURCES

Read industry magazines such as Billboard, Spin *and* Rolling Stone.

Recording Industry Association of America/RIAA
202/775-0101
www.riaa.com
Reports the latest trends on packaging, format and music sales by genre.

WEB SITES

Music Connection
www.musicconnection.com

Record Labels on the Web
www.rlabels.com

Universal Music Group
www.universalstudios.com/music

RECORD COMPANIES

Rock Art, *a book by Spencer Drake, has information on CD design.*

SURFACE DESIGN

by Constance Smith

Surface design is a commercial art form in which the final product from the designer is a pattern, usually executed on paper, ready for application to the final commercial product, often fabric for sheets, pillows, wall hangings and other items.

Because of the commercial/industrial nature of surface pattern design, the designer must understand how the fabric or paper is to be printed, how it will be merchandised in a store, and how the final product is to be used by the consumer. Surface pattern design schools and programs offer curricula that cover the technical aspects as well as the fine-art discipline needed to be a competent designer. Fine-art skills such as drawing, proportion, perspective and color theory are as necessary as technical information regarding repeats, printing and production. Very often, artists from other disciplines can cross the line into this form of design— however, not without some training and work.

Designs can be for two-dimensional surfaces such as bedding, shower curtains, wallpaper, upholstery fabric, wrapping paper, children's sleep wear, tablecloths, etc. Usually these are printed goods, but they can be a woven towel or tablecloth too.

Designers can work in the surface design industry in a variety of ways:

➤ One can work as a staff designer for a company in-house, hired by the company on a full-time or part-time basis, or as a free-lance designer who designs originals and sells the artwork, sometimes through an art rep. One could also do custom work for a specific project.

➤ In the textile and surface design industry, licensing agreements are generally negotiated for an entire line or collection. A licensing agreement for domestics would include sheets, pillowcases, duvets, shams; a license for bath products would include mats, curtains, shower curtains, accessories, towels.

Figuring out technically how to have a towel match a sheet, how to paint the artwork using less colors or screens is a big task. There are always limitations and product direction to consider, which takes experience and schooling.

ROYALTIES

Royalties generally range from 2 - 10% of wholesale, the majority being at 5% but some as low as a fraction of a percent (on very high volumes). Advances can be as high as $5000 per program.

➤ Generally, artists find reps to make their deals.

➤ Often, artists receive name credit somewhere on the product for their design: i.e., on the salvage of the fabric or the label of a sheet.

TRADE SHOW

Surtex
George Little Management
914/421-3200
www.surtex.com
The main show to exhibit surface design artwork. This show allows you to license your work directly to manufacturers. Held in May concurrently with the National Stationery Show in New York City.

ORGANIZATIONS

The Paisley Group
PO Box 40496, Pasadena, CA 91114
This is a nonprofit organization of surface pattern designers, textile artists and design representatives, organized for the purpose of providing networking, support, education and information on the issues that specifically impact these professionals.

Surface Design Association
PO Box 360, Sebastopol, CA 95473-0360
707/829-3110
www.surfacedesign.org   <surfacedesign@mail.com>
Publish a magazine entitled Survace Design Journal. *A one-year membership, which includes four issues of their magazine, is $50.*

CLASSES

The California School of Professional Fabric Design
510/549-3051
Many classes available

Image West Design
PO Box 613, San Anselmo, CA 94979-0613
415/482-9856 415/482-9857 Fax
www.imagewestdesign.com   <info@imagewestdesign.com>
Owner Teliha Draheim is a licensing agent and offers private consultations and classes. Call for free brochure.

ACTION PLAN

Use the answers to the
questions at right to create
your action plan.

1.
_____

2.
_____

3.
_____

4.
_____

5.
_____

6.
_____

7.
_____

8.
_____

9.
_____

10.
_____

List frame shops, department stores, gift shops, greeting card
stores, home décor outlets to visit to keep abreast of the
marketplace: _____

_____

_____

_____

_____

Galleries and exhibitions to attend to see new ideas and styles:

_____

_____

Products you want to see your work on: _____

_____

_____

Greeting card publishers to contact: _____

_____

_____

Print publishers to contact: _____

_____

Calendar publishers to contact: _____

_____

Miscellaneous manufacturers to contact: _____

_____

_____

Chapter 3
Legal Aspects

Copyright

Plagiarism and infringement

Issuing a license/invoice

Sample license/invoice

Delivery note

The art of the deal

Guarantees and advances

Royalty statement

Bad debts

Trademarks

Less is more.
> *Mies Van Der Rohe*

COPYRIGHT

You own the copyright to all the work you produce whether you sell the originals or not.

Copyright provides protection for an artist who has created an original work of art—pictorial, graphic or sculptural. Under the copyright law of 1976, any work created on or after January 1, 1978 is protected by common-law copyright as soon as it is completed in some tangible form. You are not even required to put the copyright © symbol on your work to protect it. Anyone (a company, individual or organization) wishing to use the artwork must have the creator's permission in writing, i.e., a license or agreement granting specific rights.

As owner of your copyright, you have exclusive right to do (and to authorize others to do) the following:

➤ Reproduce the work in copies

➤ Prepare derivatives of the work

➤ Distribute copies to the public, by rental, lease, sale

➤ Display the copyrighted work publicly (i.e., include in a motion picture, etc.)

➤ Transfer the copyright to heirs in your will

➤ Transfer part or all of your copyright through a sale, gift, donation or trade. You must do this in writing. This is *not* the same as selling or transferring ownership of an artwork. You can sell a first reproduction right to one company, say for greeting cards, and a second reproduction right to another, say for a calendar, as long as each contract allows you to do that.

You still have to prove it is your original creation, however. So how do you do that? You could take snapshots or slides and get them printed with a date on the photo. This is some proof. But this *will not* hold up in a court case. If you don't file copyright formally with the Copyright Office in Washington, DC, you cannot sue someone for infringing your copyright, should this be necessary. When you officially register your work with the Copyright Office in Washington, DC, you become eligible to receive statutory damages and attorney's fees in case of an infringement suit.

Copyright registration costs $30 per filing; you can register as many pieces as you wish at one time for $30, providing they are all similar in style. (The copyright office wants to know they are from the same artist.) Official registration is effective upon receipt of your application.

RESOURCES

Copyright Office

Library of Congress, Copyright Office, Washington, DC 20559

202/707-3000 (information) 202/707-9100 (to request forms)

www.loc.gov/copyright

Form VA is the form you will need to register your artwork. You can download this form directly from the Internet. Two pages of instructions on how to fill out Form VA can be found in ArtNetwork's book Art Office (800/383-0677), as well as a Form VA you can photocopy for sending.

Superintendent of Documents

PO Box 371954, Pittsburgh, PA 15250

To study in detail the copyright law, obtain a copy of "Copyright Law of the United States of America" (Circular '92). $14 (check, Visa or Mastercard)

WEB SITES

Art Law Center

www.artlaws.com

Institute of Art & Law

www.ial.uk.com

Starving Artists Law

www.starvingartistslaw.com

See Chapter 4 in Art Marketing 101 *for more details about copyright.*

For works created after January 1, 1978, copyright lasts for a period of 70 years after the artist's death.

QUESTIONS ABOUT COPYRIGHT

What happens if I sell an original? Do I lose the copyright?

When an original work of art is sold, the purchaser is buying the actual picture—what is painted on the canvas or paper. No reproduction rights pass to the purchaser.

Transfer of copyright must be by the owner of the copyright (you, the artist) by means of a legal document transferring it to another person or legal entity.

Can someone who buys an original work of art reproduce the work as a greeting card or a print?

Many artists think that if someone has paid a few hundred or a few thousand dollars for an original, the buyer has a right to use the work for reproduction. This is absolutely incorrect by U.S. law. To publish, print or manufacture anything that reproduces any artwork, there must be a written agreement from the copyright owner (you, the artist) granting the interested party the right to reproduce the picture for an agreed-upon fee.

PLAGIARISM AND INFRINGEMENTS

If you come across a version of one your artworks that you think has been plagiarized by another artist, first buy a copy of the suspicious piece and compare it with your own. It must be recognizable by a layperson that the infringing artwork could not have been produced had it not been copied substantially from your own work. If this is the case, you need to consult an intellectual property lawyer to pursue the matter.

By contacting the manufacturer of the plagiarized product first, however, you can possibly resolve the matter without resorting to expensive legal action. It may be that the licensee/publisher/manufacturer has in fact licensed the artwork believing the work to be an original work of art from that artist. The artist has seen your work, possibly obtained a printed sample, copied it substantially, then licensed the work. If this is the case, by informing the publisher that he is also in breach of your copyright, you can ask him to withdraw the offending products and come to some arrangement regarding compensation.

As there are so many varying factors, it would impossible here to go into what these financial arrangements should be. One way would be, however, to establish the exact value of goods that have been sold and what profit has been made from those goods. You could then request that this profit be your compensation.

Lawyers are far more experienced at negotiating this kind of breach. If it's a major infringement involving tens of thousands of dollars, consult a lawyer. If there are large sums involved, your lawyer may work on a contingency basis where she gets a percentage of the damages. If she wins, she'll probably get her fees covered by the other side, so it costs you nothing but your time. If it's a small breach and the goods produced are less than $5,000, try to negotiate a settlement. Hiring a lawyer is expensive.

ISSUING A LICENSE/ INVOICE

Each specific use of an artist's copyright should be transferred separately. The agreement should clearly state that "all rights not specifically transferred remain the property of the licensor."

A license is a document generally issued by the licensor, often in the form of an invoice. It grants a specific right to reproduce a specific artwork for a specific product, for a specific territory, for a specific period of time, for an agreed-upon fee.

Licensors/publishers/manufacturers often issue contracts that are much more detailed than the license/invoice. You can have both a contract and a license/invoice for the same project.

➤ When granting permission for one or two designs or a small group of designs, a license/invoice is usually sufficient.

➤ For a more complicated transaction, where exclusivity and guarantees are required or where there are groups of products and a substantial sum of money involved, a contract is usually required.

It is impossible to give you a template here for an all-encompassing agreement. These contracts can be 10-12 pages long and need to be drawn up individually by a lawyer. When you get to this stage, you should really be working with an agent!

LICENSE/INVOICE DETAILS

➤ **Reference.** Numbers and descriptions or titles of each artwork

➤ **Product category.** It is important to use very specific terms here. Don't use broad generic terms such as clothing or apparel. Use T-shirt or sweatshirt—these are two separate products. If you say clothing, you are in danger of a licensee assuming he has rights you don't intend to give him. Use "plastic mugs" or "tin" or "porcelain" so you are free to license these as separate product categories.

➤ **Territory.** USA only, USA and Canada only, worldwide, etc.

➤ **Term.** 3 years is typical

➤ **Advance.** This is the advance payment you have agreed upon to offset royalties earned on product sales.

➤ **Royalty.** This is the percentage of the product sales you have agreed to accept in return for usage of your art.

SAMPLE LICENSE/INVOICE

Company Name

Address

Telephone

Web site/E-mail

Licensee _____

Address _____

Telephone _____ Web site _____ E-mail _____

Date _____ License/Invoice No _____

I hereby grant the following reproduction rights in accordance with the terms and conditions on the reverse:

• Landscape at Mt Vernon

• Roses in the Sky

• Flowers in a Basket

• Flying in the Rain

Rights granted:

• Limited-edition prints; edition of 950

• World exclusive

Royalty payments:

• $300 advance for each of four images against a royalty of 10% $1200.00

• Royalties to be paid quarterly 30 days from end of each quarter

                                                            _____

                                          TOTAL $1200.00

Payment terms: 30 days from date of invoice

TERMS AND CONDITIONS

These Terms and Conditions constitute an "Agreement" between the "Artist" and the "Client" as to the terms upon which pictures are supplied and what reproduction rights are granted. In this Agreement, "picture" shall mean original art, transparency, drawing, digital scan of picture or any other item that may be offered for the purposes of reproduction.

No variation of these Terms and Conditions set out herein shall be effective unless agreed to in writing by both parties.

1. Pictures submitted to the Client by the Artist are on approval only and must be returned within 6 weeks of submission except in those cases where permission is granted by the Artist to reproduce the pictures and a license/invoice is issued. In respect of pictures submitted where a license is granted, pictures should be returned within 6 months of delivery unless otherwise agreed.

2. Return of Pictures. The Client agrees to return all pictures, which are not subject to any license that is granted, within the agreed time and shall ensure that all necessary protection is given to pictures in transit and a delivery note listing all pictures returned is enclosed with the package.

3. The Client agrees to compensate the Artist for any loss or damage to pictures while in the Client's possession or while under the Client's control, or in the possession of printers. Such compensation shall not be less than any fee for reproduction rights and no more than the cost of recommissioning the original piece of artwork.

4. No use of the pictures may be made for any purpose whatsoever without written consent of the Artist.

a) Reproduction rights (if granted) are restricted to the use, territory and time period specified on the license/invoice.

b) Reproduction rights are personal to the Client and may not be assigned to third parties unless agreed to in writing by the Artist.

c) Any rights granted are by way of license, and no partial or other assignment of copyright shall be implied.

d) Rights granted to reproduce the picture in or on a product do not include the right to use that picture directly or indirectly in any manner in the advertising of the product unless such right is specifically granted.

5. No right will be considered granted for any picture unless the Client has paid in full the license fee. Once a license has been granted by the Artist, cancellation of such license may only be accepted if such cancellation is requested within one month of the date of issue of the license.

6 Royalties. The Client agrees to pay the Artist any royalties due under any license granted and render statements 30 days after the end of each quarter, i.e., 30 days after the last day of March, June, September and December. In the case of monthly statements, 30 days after the end of each month. Any advance paid against royalties paid to the Artist is nonreturnable, but recoupable out of royalties earned.

7. The Client agrees to supply the Artist with a minimum of two (2) copies of any product or reproduction of the picture free of charge within two (2) weeks of publication or manufacture.

8. The Artist warrants that s/he has the right to enter into this agreement and warrants that the Artwork is the Artist's original creation and has not been wholly or substantially copied from any other work or material and that the exercise of the rights by the Client will not infringe the rights of any third party.

9. No variation of these terms or conditions shall be effective unless agreed to in writing by both parties.

10. This Agreement shall automatically terminate if the Client should become insolvent, enter into liquidation or become bankrupt or should have a Receiver appointed in respect of all or any of its assets.

11. The Client agrees to put a copyright line as specified below on any product or reproduction of the picture(s) licensed by the Artist.
© date Artist's name.

12. No alterations or adaptations of a picture may be made without the express written permission of the Artist.

13. This Agreement shall be governed according to Law, and the parties agree to accept the exclusive jurisdiction of the State of …………

The previous page is one example of a license/invoice. The front side gives details of the artwork licensed, with reference numbers, details of the product, territory and term of license. Terms and conditions are printed on the reverse, thereby creating a simple contract. The terms state that the license comes into effect as soon as payment is made. If the licensee disagrees with anything then he must tell you before he pays the invoice. This simple format is quite common and works well for individual artists licensing small quantities of products.

CONTRACTS

Sometimes the licensee/publisher/manufacturer will issue a contract (a more detailed written agreement) to be signed by the licensee and the copyright owner. It is important to understand what legal implications are to be considered for any type of license in order to avoid problems that could arise should the license issued not be sufficiently comprehensive.

Merchandise licensing can be full of pitfalls for the newcomer, which is why very few artists tackle it long-term on their own (see "Locating agents" in Chapter 6, as well as the list of agents in Chapter 10). A simple license agreement isn't really suitable for major merchandise licenses as it does not cover indemnities, product liability, sell-off periods, approval procedures, access to accounts for auditing and other such matters.

It is very difficult to advise on contractual issues in any depth, as there are many aspects to consider. In some cases, the publisher's contract or agreement may be quite straightforward. However, too frequently, publishers insert a few "interesting" clauses that, if signed by you, can give them more rights than you intend. Each artist may have special needs. Expert legal advice is essential.

DELIVERY NOTE

On the following page is a basic template called a delivery note to use when sending transparencies or original art to a licensee. Print the same terms and conditions (from page 66) on the reverse of this delivery note form. It allows you to charge the licensee should she lose or damage your work. It also lays out the terms under which you are sending her the work. List all the reference numbers of work submitted, just as you would in the license/invoice.

You should know where your transparencies are at all times.

DELIVERY NOTE

Licensee _____   Artist/licensor _____

Contact name _____   Address _____

Address _____   City/State/Zip _____

City/State/Zip _____   Telephone _____

Telephone _____   E-mail _____

E-mail _____   www. _____

www. _____

Date _____

The items listed below are submitted to you under the terms and conditions listed on reverse.

Ref #	Description of piece/title	Item sent

Loss/Damage Fee: _____

Transparencies: _____

Originals: _____

Total number of transparencies submitted:

Please return the transparencies within six weeks of delivery-note date if you do not wish to use them.

THE ART OF THE DEAL

Understanding how you arrive at a royalty fee that is fair for you and the licensee/publisher/manufacturer is an important aspect of licensing. You will need some sales information in order to calculate your intended compensation.

AREAS CONTRACTS SHOULD COVER

All the categories noted below are necessary to understand in order to allow you to issue a license for the use of your work. While most publishers have a standard way of figuring this out, it is important that you get this information to enable you to understand the financial aspects of the deal and how much you can potentially earn.

➤ **Usage** - what product will be manufactured

➤ **Selling price of product** - how much royalty will be paid

➤ **Print run** - quantity that will be contracted for

➤ **Territory** - where this product will be distributed

➤ **Term** - how long this product will be marketed

USAGE

This is the product category the publisher desires to use your artwork for, i.e., limited-edition print, calendar, jigsaw, note pad, greeting card, etc. It is important to be very specific with respect to the product so the publisher cannot publish other products without your permission.

SELLING PRICE OF PRODUCT

The selling price of a product is the actual dollar amount the publisher receives for selling a print or card, i.e., the wholesale price. There could be a published price in the publisher's catalog, say $75 for a particular limited edition, but with discounts the average price could be much less.

LIMITED EDITION EXAMPLE

If a publisher produces 950 copies of a limited-edition litho using your art, and the print sells for $75 wholesale, the retail price would generally be $150.

If the edition sells out, the publisher would receive 950 x $75. He may, however, give a 10% discount if galleries buy a quantity. If he sells a small quantity to a distributor in Japan or Australia, he will have to sell these at 50% of wholesale ($37.50) to allow the distributor to sell them to a gallery in his own country at the wholesale price to make his profit.

Lets assume the publisher receives 950 x $50 (average sale price), or a total of $47,500. At a royalty rate of 10%, you would receive $4750. With a 15% royalty, your revenue would be $7125. If four editions are produced each year, that would be $28,500—a nice income for four prints.

Don't forget: this is potential revenue. Editions have to sell out for you to receive the full payment.

GREETING CARD EXAMPLE

The publisher initially prints 5000 cards. The publisher sells each one at 75¢. His potential sales are therefore 5000 x 75¢, or $3750. The publisher can initially afford to pay you around $225—6% of $3750. Since greeting-card royalty rates vary from 4-8%, 6% is a good royalty rate.

The publisher may, in fact, sell 10,000 cards in a three-year period. So how do you deal with this? Every publisher will have his own fee system based on his average sales per design. If you sell a group of designs, then a royalty-based fee is by far the best way to maximize your earnings, even if the advance is low. A $200-300 advance is quite normal against 5%.

Greeting-card publishers will require exclusive rights for cards in a territory. Try to stick to the US and Canada only, as many publishers sell very little abroad. The rights could then be sold in the UK and other countries if the work is suitable, giving you additional income. Large corporations, however, may insist on world card rights as their overseas sales may be substantial.

If you sell only one or two designs to a card publisher, it may be better for you and the publisher to agree on a flat fee. To administer royalties on just one or two designs may not be cost-effective. From your point of view, it's much better to have your entire fee up front than to receive a check for $5.75 per quarter over a three-year period!

FLAT FEE NEGOTIATIONS

A flat fee should be based on average sales over the term of the license. For example: Average sale is 12,000 cards over 3 years at 75¢, or $9,000. At a royalty rate of 5%, the flat fee would be $450; at 6% it would be $540.

As the publisher is paying up front and there is no guarantee that he will sell 12,000, he'll try to settle for even a lower percentage, say 4%, or $360. You should negotiate for $400, which is half-way between and fair for both.

Use this flat fee example for any product. Remember, though, that royalty rates vary from product to product, as well as from publisher to publisher.

THE PRINT RUN

The third determining factor in calculating an appropriate royalty fee is the quantity of any given edition.

In the limited-edition market of lithographic reproductions, 950 is about the maximum quantity that has been established as a norm. Many arguments have come forward as to what the maximum quantity should be; it is very subjective. If a company wants to bring out a special edition on a subject they feel is going to be a major seller, then there is nothing to stop them producing a limited edition of 5000. This can only be justified in very special circumstances. Quite often, it can be abused in the name of profiteering. The whole concept of limited editions is just that—the edition is limited so that it is rare and therefore collectable.

ARTIST'S PROOFS

The publishing industry's norm is to produce no more than 10% of the edition as artist's proofs. In the early days, this part of the edition was reserved for the artist. This, however, was when editions were handmade originals. These days, artists proofs are a way the publisher can produce extra copies to sell. The artist can expect to get five to 10 proofs of an edition. If you can negotiate more, then great. The rest of the proofs go to the publisher. This should be agreed upon at the outset and put in the written and signed agreement.

There are a number of collectors who only collect artist's proofs. Some actually collect particular numbers. Selling to these buyers at a higher price can prove quite valuable to the publisher. The artist's royalties on these prints will be a little higher.

TERRITORY

The geographic territory covered by your contract is an important factor.

In the case of limited-edition prints, the territory would normally be worldwide in order to allow the publisher to sell to any gallery that wished to purchase the print.

Let's use an example of a poster with an unlimited print run. If the publisher's distribution chain is the US and Canada only, the contract should be exclusive to that area, and your license should say exactly that. This allows you to sell this particular artwork as a poster in the UK, Australia, or wherever you can find a publisher to license it.

It should be apparent that by limiting territories, it is possible to generate several income streams on one design, not only for different products but for the same product in different territories. This is a crucial point and must not be overlooked. Many publishers try to obtain world rights even if they don't distribute worldwide! You could earn far more by licensing the design to a licensee/publisher/manufacturer in each territory.

In the print and poster industry, many companies do in fact sell worldwide. It is important to ask them: Don't give away territories unless there are potential sales for the licensee in those territories.

THE TERM

The term is the length of time you allow the publisher to use the artwork. It is always important to specify this in the contract. Three years is normal. If the licensee/publisher/manufacturer wants more time, she can have an option to renew for an additional three years when the term ends. This way, if you are earning a satisfactory income, you would be pleased to renew her license. If the design is not selling, then the publisher would decline a renewal, leaving the design clear and free. If there is no term set, you have effectively given the publisher indefinite use, which must always be avoided.

THE TRUTH OF THE MATTER

One company said that its policy was to buy world porcelain mug rights for a flat fee of $250. A company rep then showed me a design he'd purchased and told me proudly that he'd sold over one million mugs of this particular design. If the mug only sold for a $1 wholesale, at 5% royalty that would have given the artist $50,000. No wonder he didn't want to pay a royalty. And no wonder I wouldn't sell him any designs for a $250 flat fee!

GUARANTEES AND ADVANCES

Royalties are always based on the net amount the publisher receives, not the retail price the consumer pays.

As a rule, you want to negotiate an advance against royalties. This way, if sales are high, you benefit. If sales are low, the publisher isn't paying out large sums of unearned money.

When you have a range of designs to sell—which means you have put in a great deal of work to create the concept—it is quite normal to ask for a minimum guarantee each year, particularly if these designs are to be used on several products.

ADVANCE AGAINST ROYALTIES

An advance against royalties is the initial fee received against a percentage of royalty payments that will be due on the sale of products. It should be indicated in the written agreement that advances are nonrefundable, protecting you if the product is not marketed well.

Be aware that a product takes time to manufacture. It then needs to be marketed and sold at trade shows. This could take six to twelve months from the date of the license.

EXCLUSIVITY

A manufacturer wants to produce greeting cards, notelets, magnets, ring binders, journals and one or two other gift items. He needs 24 designs initially, which he will use on greeting cards. Some of these he will also use on other products. He may also need some individual designs produced for products with unusual shapes or that need to be in landscape format (wider than tall). Since he is producing a major range, he wants to protect his market: He therefore wants exclusivity. He may insist that he is the exclusive licensee in these product categories. This could be good if the product line sells very well, but if it's a flop, how do you protect yourself?

First you need to determine the potential earnings for the entire project. Be quite open about this when discussing the matter with the publisher. If he offers you $10,000 advance against 6%, but wants three years' rights and total exclusivity for your work in these product areas, it may sound like a good deal, but if that's all you end up with because the product doesn't sell, then you've effectively tied yourself to an agreement for three years in several major product categories, which only brings in $3333 per year.

There are several ways to negotiate this kind of deal:

➤ If the publisher is confident that she'll meet certain sales targets (let's say $250,000 minimum per year in sales) then at 6% this would give you $15,000 per year in royalties. Suggest this as the minimum guarantee for each of the three years, with an advance of $10,000 at the outset and $10,000 at the commencement of each year. She would, of course, need to pay you any royalties due over and above the initial advance when they were due. This, in effect, guarantees you at least $10,000 a year even if the publisher doesn't meet her target for each year.

➤ If he will **not** commit to a guarantee, the next best thing is to simply grant exclusivity on those designs he chooses, as opposed to exclusivity on you as an artist in those product areas. This may not be acceptable to him, particularly if the style is easily recognizable. His argument will be that if he spends a great deal on manufacturing product and then another publisher offers you a deal to produce a new range, there could potentially be two similar ranges competing in the marketplace. One way around this predicament is to grant exclusivity on that particular style so as not to cause any conflict. This would leave you free to produce work in different styles and subject matter and license it to other manufacturers.

➤ Ultimately, you need a deal that suits both parties and doesn't tie you into exclusivity (unless the publisher is prepared to give you a minimum guarantee). If you find yourself in this situation, it usually means the publisher really likes your work, so don't be bullied into what may sound like a great license, only to find that you are locked into a deal that isn't producing income and denies you the right to sell to other companies. This happens far more often than one would think.

ROYALTY RATES

➤ The more well-known the artist, the higher the royalty.

➤ The more exclusive the contract, the higher the royalty.

QUESTIONS TO ASK

➤ What will be the actual selling price of the product?

➤ What discounts are given?

➤ What is your return policy?

➤ When is the licensor credited for the sale and when is he paid?

➤ If the retailer does not pay, is that percentage deducted from the artist's royalties?

To verify that your royalties are being paid properly, within your agreement should be a clause that states that you can examine the licensee's books. Insist on being paid late fees and interest if payments are delayed.

SUMMING UP

From the information you have gathered, you can assess whether the fee suggested by the publisher is fair. If you are offered $200 for a greeting card design with an average sale of 12,000 at 75¢, i.e., $9000, then you know that you are being offered only a little over 2%. An educated artist (you!) will know that is too low.

Negotiating is not an easy job, but using the system laid out here will give you enough information to know why you are negotiating, helping you negotiate with confidence. It shows the publisher you are not someone to be bamboozled into accepting a lower fee than you justly deserve. Use common sense. You know what you want—go for it!

Once you get into even more complicated licensing deals and contracts, you might seek the services of a good licensing agent.

Remember:

➤ License the exclusive rights only on artwork the publisher wants to use.

➤ Get all the information as outlined above (usage, territory, etc.) to determine your fees.

➤ Find out if the publisher has a set fee structure, i.e., "She won't budge."

➤ Sub-license agreements are sometimes included, which in effect give the publisher rights to license your designs himself. Unless you want him to do this, the sub-license agreement should be deleted from any agreement.

➤ Contracts should always be reviewed by a lawyer who is educated in intellectual property law. At rates of $150 - 350 per hour for a good attorney, this is not really cost-effective or practical for a small contract. However, if you are unhappy with an aspect of the contract, it is always safer in the long run to get legal advice rather than commit to something you don't fully understand.

➤ Be careful before signing contracts. Read them thoroughly. Mark any areas you do not understand and get advice or discuss it with the publisher. You must understand fully what you are signing. Feel free to make any amendments that are needed.

➤ Do not be afraid to stick to your guns if there is something in the agreement you do not like. In many cases, publishers have a standard all-encompassing contract. If the contract includes rights you don't wish to give to the publisher, then delete these items and initial the deletions.

➤ **Promotional approvals:** written approval must be given before a licensee can use your image or artwork in any special advertisements featuring your work. It's a good idea to let them do this, but you want to have some say in how it is executed. Obviously, your work can appear in product catalogs automatically.

➤ **Artist's credit:** to guarantee that you receive credit on product as well as in advertising, it must be specifically included in agreement.

➤ **Guarantee:** provides the artist with a certain level of revenue in royalties no matter what the amount of sales turn out to be. Guarantees are often linked to option clauses: the license agreement is for a certain number of years, and if the artist has earned a certain amount of money through royalties, the licensee has the right automatically to extend the term of the license. If not, then renewal is at the discretion of the artist. These options are sometimes called performance criteria.

➤ **Quality approval:** an artist receives the right to approve a final sample. This is essential in the case of limited-edition prints. However, on certain licenses for products such as greeting cards it is not necessary for licenses to have approval procedures for any single design. Use common sense.

➤ When your contract ends, it is customary to grant your licensee/ publisher/manufacturer a "sell-off" period of three to six months in order to sell stock on hand. After this periods he should, however, be made to destroy any stocks he has left, or offer it to you at cost or renew the license.

TIPS

➤ How are you paid: royalty or flat fee? Royalties may take a long time to dribble in.

➤ If paid in royalties, do you get an advance? Try to negotiate a nonreturnable advance.

➤ Will they want to buy the original artwork? Try to keep it if possible. The value will increase as the reproduction becomes successful.

➤ Will they provide insurance while the artwork is in transit?

➤ Will they pay for shipping?

➤ What kind of promotion do they provide? Catalogs? Mailings?

➤ How large will the edition be?

➤ Number of artist's proofs? How will they be signed and numbered? Does the publisher require any artist's proofs for sale?

➤ Number of printer's proofs for use as documentation and for promotion and exhibition purposes? Usually these are not marketed. These proofs can be stamped on the reverse side in large letters to identify them as printer's proofs. Provide for one printer's proof to become the property of the printer pulling the edition. All plates should be preserved in their cancelled states for art historical purposes. The contract should specify whether such plates are to be the property of the artist or the publisher.

➤ All trial proofs that are not destroyed should be the property of the artist and should be delivered to the artist on or before the date of publication of the edition.

➤ Specify return of transparencies to the artist after printing.

➤ Provide for delivery to the artist of a cancellation proof showing that the plate has been destroyed or otherwise rendered unusable for further printing.

ROYALTY STATEMENT

Read your royalty statement carefully. Check for errors—they happen quite often. Make sure you receive a royalty statement every quarter, within 30 days of the end of each quarter. If it doesn't arrive, inquire as to why.

Make your terms (when you require payment on invoice/license) 30 days from date of invoice/license. If you haven't received payment after 30 days, call the accounts payable department.

ARTIST ROYALTY STATEMENT

1/1/XX - 3/30/XX

000654   Artist name   CONTRACT # XXXC

Address

Series	Title	Description	Total sales
STM	567	Lilies	$3879.02
		Royalty at 10%	387.90
		Less advance	-0-
		Royalty due	**$ 387.90**
AST	133	Windows on Paris	$2899.03
		Royalty at 8%	231.92
		Less advance	-0-
		Royalty due	**$ 231.92**
		Total enclosed	**$619.82**

BAD DEBTS

Freelance artists should be paid promptly. If you are having to wait long periods for money due, talk to the art director or your contact at the company and try to explain that if you do work for them, you need to be paid according to the terms that have been agreed upon. If you have to accept 60 days, then it should not be longer. Thirty days should be the norm, however.

If an account goes beyond 90 - 120 days past due, you should give a final warning. By far, the easiest way is:

➤ A seven-day written warning

➤ A phone call to the accounts payable department

➤ If no result, then proceed to put your claim through the Small Claims Court. This avoids lawyer's costs and is a fairly simple process. You fill out a form, attach a copy of the invoice, pay a fee to the court, and they issue a demand for payment. The court will advise you on what to do next if you still do not receive payment.

➤ You could consider a collection agency. They will normally take a percentage of the amount collected. This is an alternative to the small claims court and can be quite effective.

Hopefully you will rarely need to do this! You may lose the customer, but who needs licensees who don't pay?

If you are in the unfortunate position of experiencing delays in payments, send a copy of your original invoice/license along with a note similar to the one below.

PAST DUE NOTICE

My records indicate that my Invoice/License No..............

dated................... for $300.00 has not been paid. My terms

are 30 days from the date of the invoice, and I respectfully

request that you send payment by return mail.

TRADEMARKS

Should you invent a name for a concept, cartoon or any other project, it is possible to protect this name by registering it as a trademark. A trademark is essentially a non-generic word or words such as Rug Rats, Teletubbies, etc., which you wish to protect by formal registration through the United States Patent and Trademark Office.

Trademarking is essential if you have a successful merchandise program you want to protect against infringers and pirates. Although piracy still exists, it is impossible to protect your trademarks against such infringements without proper registration.

Most illustrators find this a very daunting prospect. Advice is always needed in these matters. It is possible that major clients with whom you are working will contribute to or even pay for these costs. They might wait until the project is assigned to them, however. (Remember: if the items are registered in their name, you no longer own them. Don't let them do this!)

There are search facilities available through which you can see if your trademark has been registered. You can also search for similar registered tradmarks that could conflict with yours. This can be done by yourself or through a patent and trademarks lawyer.

Registration can be quite expensive, as it normally involves various registrations for different product categories. If you want to register the trademark for different countries, there is a fee for each country. Costs depend on the number and nature of countries designated. A typical fee for the UK, for instance, is $630.

RESOURCES

United States Patent and Trademark Office
Crystal Plaza 3, Room 2C02, Washington, DC 20231
800/786-9199 703/308-4357
Provides information and forms on how to register a trademark. Application fee @ $325; renewal fee @ $400

ACTION PLAN

Use the answers to the questions at right to create your action plan.

1. _____

2. _____

3. _____

4. _____

5. _____

6. _____

7. _____

8. _____

9. _____

10. _____

❏ Prepare Form VA to register your artwork with the copyright office.

❏ Create a delivery note form.

❏ Create a license/invoice form.

❏ Locate a lawyer knowledgable in intellectual property

RECOMMENDED READING

Licensing Art & Design by Caryn R Leland will help you figure out what your contract should contain. It's available through your local bookstore, library or directly from the publisher, Allworth Press, at 212/777-8395. ISBN: 1-880559-27-7

Chapter 4

Business Practices

Identifying your artwork

Copyright control cards

Keeping clear records

Photographing your artwork

Truth exists, only lies are invented.

Georges Braque

IDENTIFYING YOUR WORK

To stand any chance of success in the industry, you must go about establishing specific business practices to ensure that you don't run into complex problems once your activity starts booming.

COPYRIGHT CONTROL

You must always insist that any goods reproduced using your artwork are marked with a copyright symbol, " ©," the date, and your name.

© 2002 John Doe

➤ Make sure this information, © 2002 John Doe, is given to any publisher or manufacturer and is on every item of work, transparency, etc.

➤ Make sure this is stated in your agreement.

CATALOGING ARTWORK

Whether it be the sale of originals via galleries or licensing reproduction rights to fine art publishers, greeting card publishers, calendar manufacturers, etc., you must establish specific business practices to ensure that you have a simple, easy-to-run system of cataloging your work. A simple way to keep track of each artwork that you produce is using index cards, available in a multitude of colors, to help you color-code your work.

➤ Give each artwork a code, such as JD (for John Doe, i.e., your own initials) plus a number. Start with 01 and work numerically from this point, i.e., JD/01, JD/02, etc.

➤ You will need the title and a general description of the image on the index card as well. Remember that after 11 years' time you may not recall every picture. If a picture is returned without its number or caption, you will want to be able to identify it easily and accurately.

➤ Record every artwork you produce. Stick a label on the back of the piece with the reference number, or if on art board or paper, write it on the back. Include the date of completion.

If you are sending transparencies to a licensee or agent, place a copyright symbol with your name on the tranny cover, e.g., © John Doe 2001, the title, reference number (which coincides with the original reference number), address and telephone number. You can also add the words "all rights reserved" if you like.

Put labels on the plastic covers of your trannies.

John Doe

19 Knox St, SF, CA 94941

415/678-9999

© 2002 John Doe 10/01

Still Life Roses   JD/01

Every time you issue a licence/invoice, *you must*, prior to issuing it, pull out your index card for the piece of work you are licensing. Fill out all the details of the license/invoice as follows:

➤ Date of invoice

➤ Invoice number

➤ Rights granted

➤ Term

➤ Territory

➤ Publisher

➤ Fee charged

➤ Royalty rate

➤ Date license ends

COPYRIGHT CONTROL CARDS

Purchase a copy of Art Office, *published by ArtNetwork. It contains business forms and legal documents to help you get and stay organized. Call 800/383-0677.*

COPYRIGHT CONTROL CARD

Title: Still Life Roses   **Date of copyright registration** 3/4/00   **Job #:** JD/01

Description: Blue vase with four roses against a pink background on white tablecloth with apple on left and rose petal on right

Medium Oil on canvas   **Size** 12x15"   **Completed** October 1, 2002

Original work sold on _/ _/0_ to:_____, address _____

_____ tele_____e-mail_____

Usage rights:

• **Invoice # XXX-123002**   Date 12/30/02   World rights
  Limited-edition print (350)   Advance of $ 300   Against royalty of 10%
  Martin Publishing

• **Invoice # XXX-010802**   Date 1/8/02   U.S. rights 3 years
  Jigsaw   Advance of $ 300   Against royalty of 8%
  Puzzling Publishers   Expires 1/8/05

KEEPING CLEAR RECORDS

Paper tracking becomes a very important aspect of your business as you receive more and more licensing contracts. It is imperative that you operate a job card system to keep track of all your submissions and contracts.

When you send out transparencies, slides, CDs or scans, send a delivery note (see page 68) with the items listed. This delivery note can act as a job card, which records who has what and when it was delivered. Keep a photocopy of each delivery note in a file separated by month. This way, you can go back the next month and contact licensees/publishers/agents who have not responded to your submission, as well as keep records of their response.

Transparencies, slides and originals cost money. Not only that, but it takes time to get the product prepared. If publishers lose one, they need to be charged an appropriate fee. The delivery note has a space at the bottom so you can fill in the replacement cost before you send work.

Over time, you may, in fact, invoice the same original artwork for different uses by several licensees (as in the sample copyright control card). These records are your complete history of the reproduction rights given for each artwork. Can you imagine if things got confused? What a mess! These records also help prevent you from invoicing a reproduction twice, as well as knowing whether the design is available for a particular usage. A publisher may also ask if the design has been used before. Without proper records, this would be very hard to remember. Recordkeeping, as you can see, is extremely important. Never put it off. Always fill in the copyright control card prior to typing up your invoice—this way you won't make a mistake.

REISSUING INVOICES

Despite the fact that a design has become free after three years (after being used as a jigsaw with Company X), if Company Y wants to use the same design for a jigsaw, even though the design is technically available, you must inform Company Y of the previous usage.

➤ Firstly, the design has just been on the market as a jigsaw. Company Y, the new manufacturer, may have a similar customer base to Company X, in which case Company Y most certainly wouldn't want the design.

➤ Secondly, Company Y may simply not want a design his competitor has used. If he's happy knowing the design has been used previously by a competitor, then there is not a problem. Company Y must have the choice. Some companies are fierce competitors. Ignore this advice at your own peril; this is simply good business practice and proves you are a genuine and professional artist. Licensees will respect you for informing them.

TIPS

➤ Don't forget to pull out the copyright control card and cancel the entry if a job is cancelled. This is easy to overlook. A few months or years later, you could end up thinking you've licensed a piece, when in fact you haven't.

➤ When you have invoiced a few hundred artworks and have been running your system for awhile, you will also see an additional value to this index card system as artworks become available again. As contracts expire, you can reissue new licenses for the same artwork. It will be easy to recognize when this is about to occur as you review your copyright control card.

WIN-WIN SITUATION

Take your partnerships with licensees and publishers further than the next artist. Build a relationship that is mutually beneficial to both parties. Stay in contact with your agent. Ask what is happening in the marketplace (you already know a bit but are always wanting to know more). Find out what they would like to see from you: size, colors, etc. Get your projects to them early—what a relief that would be to them! You shouldn't be surprised that they then bring you into their business plans more and more.

PHOTOGRAPHING YOUR ARTWORK

Your objective should be to ensure that you protect your future income in case an original is sold, stolen or destroyed. You must have a professional reproduction-quality transparency, scan, slide or photo print (all four are preferable) of your original work. Publishers generally do not work from a 35mm; they most often work from a scan or transparency. Keep this in mind as you sell your pieces. As they leave your premises, you need a properly taken scan or transparency.

In some cases where the art is being published at a very high standard, the publisher will want to photograph from the original in order to ensure the best possible reproduction of the work. If you send an original (or leave an original with a publisher), be sure to put its full value on your invoice, with a note for its return.

Even if you've sold your original, you should be keeping track of who the owner is (note space on copyright control card for such information). You should also know where s/he currently lives—s/he should be on your invitation/purchaser/client mailing list. Even if they live clear across the country, you should be sending them an invitation to your shows (they will be impressed). In this manner, you can keep track of them should they move again.

TRANSPARENCIES

You need to have duplicates or even triplicates of all your trannies. If you have scans, be sure to back them up and store them off-site.

A transparency ("tranny" or "four-by-five (4x5)" for short) is by far the best way to preserve your work. It is the format most widely used by publishers for reproduction. The most common size for a tranny is 4x5". It is possible to make duplicates ("dupe" for short). Make sure a dupe is made from an original transparency. A dupe of a dupe loses quality significantly.

The most important factor is getting a **professional** tranny made. Prices for trannies range from $15 - 35. You may get a deal as low as $12 if you have several pieces photographed at the same time. Most professional labs in major cities offer this service. Take time to make friends with your local lab. See if you can get a special price by being a regular customer and bringing in batches of at least six pieces at a time.

Store trannies in the sleeves they come in from the lab. Don't forget to label them appropriately (page 84) before sending them out.

SCANS

A scan is a computer-generated copy of an original artwork. You need a scan with 1200 dots per inch/dpi resolution so that the image can eventually be produced to a large size. Be forewarned: this takes up a fair amount of disk space on a computer.

If your original work is 20x24" or larger, it is possible to have it scanned digitally at a lab. Doing it without professional equipment can create problems. You need proper studio setup to achieve good results—it's imperative to get the work absolutely square as well as properly lit.

You can make a scan from a tranny, but the more steps removed you are from the original artwork, the less true the colors will be.

If you have the appropriate computer equipment, you can use the scans the lab has made to print color copies on your office color printer. This color laser can be a cost-effective way to send samples of your work.

35MM SLIDES

Less expensive to produce than transparencies, slides are best for small reproductions—greeting cards, books. While it is possible to reproduce from a good quality 35mm, it is not advisable. They do not blow up well when made larger than 8x10". Since many prints are much larger than this, you will need to have a scan or transparency, or you might lose a chance of publishing a work.

RESOURCES

Print File Inc
PO Box 607638, Orlando, FL 32860-7638
407/886-3100 407/886-0008 Fax
www.printfile.com <support@printfile.com>
Sells materials to protect and organize your slides and transparencies.

Visual Horizons
180 Metro Park, Rochester, NY 14623
800/424-1011
www.storesmart.com <info@storesmart.com>
Duplicate slides, produce scans from slides, and more.

Slides can be fine for sending to a publisher in a portfolio as a sample of your work. If you send laser copies that are not necessary for them to return, just write a note: "samples only - need not be returned."

Sleeves/covers from a photo lab are generally made from material that doesn't affect the transparency. Some manufactured sleeves can actually "sweat" and damage the transparency.

ACTION PLAN

Use the answers to the questions at right to create your action plan.

1.
_____

2.
_____

3.
_____

4.
_____

5.
_____

6.
_____

7.
_____

8.
_____

9.
_____

10.
_____

❏ Place a copyright symbol and your name on all your artwork.

❏ Prepare a job card for every artwork produced, with a reference number, date produced and any other details such as size, medium and a good description.

❏ Have artwork scanned.

❏ Have artwork reproduced as 4x5" transparencies.

❏ Make duplicates/triplicates of all 4x5s.

❏ Create an easy-to-locate filing system for 4x5s.

❏ Label all 4x5s.

Chapter 5
Presentations

Market research

Presentation know-how

New modes of submission

Telephone contact

Trade shows

Showing up is 90% of the success.
Woody Allen

MARKET RESEARCH

It's amazing how many submissions are sent to publishers and licensees by artists who have given no thought whatsoever to the content of the work and the needs of the company receiving it. Each publisher or licensee is unique. Presentations should be geared specifically to the person or company you are approaching. Before you submit anything, you must understand the market sector you are targeting. Do the basic research. Look smart—study your market.

TREND SPOTTING

Trends can be created by several sources; fashion and home furnishings are two. These industries plan one or two years ahead. They each have color guides, which originate from market research and forecasts. These color-trend guides are not available to the public and cost hundreds of dollars to purchase.

Such guides prove that a great deal of thought goes into fashion trends in the marketplace. Framed prints reflect this by being complementary to home furnishing fabrics. *Décor* magazine publishes a color guide each year, which can be very helpful if you are in the print market (see magazine section in Chapter 10).

Other trends just start with an innovative company putting out a range of cards or gift products that catch the consumers' attention. Suddenly there is a rush to follow by many other publishers who want to "ride the wave" before the fad becomes worn out and passé.

TIPS

➤ Don't be overly ambitious at first. Choose only half a dozen professionals to pursue at the outset. Learn the tricks of the trade—how to talk, what to send.

➤ Target your market carefully, understand the clients' needs as best you can. Look carefully at what you do, and relate your work to a particular product that fits well.

➤ Listen to the market. If you give it what it wants, you will be successful.

Always spend a portion of your time searching for new art buyers, whether it be visiting stores, trade shows, via the Internet or art buyer guides. Ideally, use all four methods and you'll soon have a great customer list.

Send the companies you choose to market to exactly what they want. It's not good to send, for instance, textile designs or nude figure studies to a print publisher who only prints wildlife. Although this may seem obvious to some, it's amazing how often this happens!

An approach to several industries at once may appear rather ambitious to some. Perhaps your subject matter may only relate to stationery and greeting cards. If that's the case, then choose publishers from those industries to start.

GET TO KNOW YOUR MARKET

➤ Read magazines on art, fashion and interior decor (listed in Chapter 10).

➤ Read magazines pertaining directly to the licensing market (listed in Chapter 10).

➤ Visit art exhibitions, fashion shows, interior design exhibitions.

➤ Visit trade shows as often as possible (listed in Chapter 10).

➤ Observe current events and sociological trends.

➤ Research licensees and publishers via the Internet.

➤ Visit stores to see what is being sold.

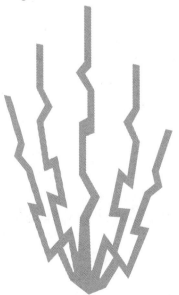

Research will need to continue throughout your career.

Names and addresses of manufacturers are often on the actual product, i.e., on the back of greeting cards, in the frontispiece of a book, the label of a pillow.

PRESENTATION KNOW-HOW

Solely having good artwork is not enough to enter the publishing and licensing market. You need to have a concept about how your artwork would be striking on a particular product.

Marketing your work is a matchmaking process.

To have any success in licensing, whether it be in an artist brand, artwork-as-brand, or individual licenses, you will need to have a strategy.

➤ Define your artwork: Is it appropriate for commercial use on products?

➤ Select a product line where your work can best be used. Research companies who currently work with that product line.

➤ Understand your competition; position the uniqueness of your art style into place.

➤ You will need to be willing to let go of your art. Will you be offended if your painting is on a shower curtain? Make sure you understand your psychological limits before you go forward.

➤ You will have to accept commercial standards of reproduction. No reproduction can be exactly like the original. Only so much time and effort is spent on getting a greeting card to be a "perfect" reproduction; more time is spent on getting a limited edition to be "perfect," however.

➤ Can you take the pressure of a commission—and deliver on time?

➤ Will you be able to accept art direction—perhaps cropping of your artwork?

SERIES

Prepare a series of artworks that you wish to license. To do this, you need to study the market, educate yourself and come up with a series of designs targeted at a particular segment of the market. Focus on a small group of products to begin with, which eventually can be licensed to a small number of licensees. These initial products should be the ones most ideally suited for the art you have produced.

PROTOTYPES

Create some presentation boards of the actual product or ideas for products that you have. This way you can see how the design works on the actual item. It may need a special border, a background, logo, graphics. What about packaging?

By completing this exercise, you may find that your artwork is not strong enough or might not work quite right. It allows you to see what the licensee/publisher/manufacturer has to do to create a product that sells.

You may be saying right now, "Look. I'm not a designer!" That may well be true, but if you want to work in a particular market sector, it behooves you to understand some of the basic principles of product design. It's not just a question of slapping a picture on the product. Background colors, borders, logo: they all play an important part in creating a product that is punchier and more sellable. You want it to say "pick me up." You need to know how this is done.

Getting the first licenses are the hardest part; after that you get on a roll.

In our own studio, we actually produced an entire campaign on a particular teddy bear project we handled. In the studio, the mock-ups looked great, but when they were put next to a range of new Disney products or some new flavor-of-the-moment merchandise such as the Teletubbies, which were all very vibrant primary colors, our delicate, soft pastels looked absolutely lost. Had the product been manufactured, we'd have had an absolute failure on our hands. We therefore increased the intensity of the borders and created a much stronger design concept, which stood up well next to the competition.

MAILERS

In this day and age with computers, color laser copies and inexpensive color printers, it is rather easy to create a simple letter-size (8.5x11") flyer showing examples of your work.

All you need is several scans of your artwork at 300dpi. If you have slides and no scan, go to a local copy shop or quick-print shop. Scanning might cost about $4 per transparency or $2 per slide. Have your name, address, phone number and a few details about yourself and the subject matter typeset on the flyer and you have an inexpensive form of promotional material.

RECIPIENTS' RESPONSE

Keep your presentation simple; show your best work. Straightforward, no-nonsense presentations on letter-size sheets seem to ultimately show

Letter-size format is by far the best—it fits into files easily.

the work in its best light. More elaborate presentations can take several minutes to open—too long for some people! Remember, your main goal is to have the art buyer call or write you to ask to see more.

➤ When sending slides, use a plastic slide sleeve. Slides individually wrapped and taped to a piece of card can take 10 minutes to unwrap and review. Not fun!

➤ Concertina books, boxes of slides with a little viewer, tubes with dozens of rolled-up laser prints (rolled so tight they won't lie flat)—these are perhaps eye-catching but also very frustrating, even a downright nuisance in some cases.

TIPS

➤ The content of the mailer/presentation is very important. The art director/buyer may receive up to 10 presentations a day, so you want to ensure that yours stands out.

➤ The work must be good and targeted well to the licensee's needs.

➤ The work needs to be displayed well. If you are aiming at the card market, you could make up card samples, for instance.

BIOS

If you are approaching the commercial market of greeting cards, prints, posters, gift ware, jigsaws, calendars, etc., including a bio in your presentation is not necessary. If, however, you've had experience with some big licensees, you might want to mention them in your cover letter. Generally, let the artwork speak for itself. Buyers are really not interested in your history unless it has some great significance.

If you are entering the more refined markets, such as fine art limited editions, a short bio is quite important.

A SHORT BIO SHOULD INCLUDE:

➤ Date of birth

➤ **Art education:** give only relevant info (no one wants to know how many high school certificates you have or that you once played basketball)

➤ **Significant commissions**: any clients you've worked for in the past who may be known to the person you're contacting.

➤ **Collections your work is in**: noteworthy galleries, museums or well-known collectors

➤ **Statement:** Your approach to or philosophy of art. Keep it to one short paragraph.

MAILING OUT YOUR PRESENTATION

➤ Keep a current database on all potential licensees, either on computer or on an index card system.

➤ Make sure you have the correct contact person. Before sending out any presentation, telephone the client and ask to speak to the art department/art buyer/art director. If you can't get through to that person, explain to the recipient that you are about to send in some samples of your artwork and you'd like to know to whom they should be addressed.

➤ When you call the art director, ask what format the company prefers for artwork submissions, and what styles and themes the manufacturer is looking for presently.

➤ Be sure to note your web site address (URL) so they can review your pieces on-line if desired.

➤ Send a letter with your mailer/presentation stating that you are a free-lance artist, and this is the style/standard of work you produce. If you are able to produce other styles, explain in a simple manner what else you can do. Whatever you decide to say in your letter, keep it simple and not too long. Remember, this may be the 50th presentation this week the art director has reviewed.

➤ Some publishers have buying periods, so it's best to submit during the time suggested or your work could lie in a filing cabinet until the review dates.

When submitting work or making an inquiry, always enclose a SASE—self-addressed stamped envelope.

97

NEW MODES OF SUBMISSION

The Internet allows for quick communications. You can send images anywhere in the world in seconds!

The Internet has changed and will continue to change our lives. As more and more people become computer literate, it will become the accepted way to view portfolios. Learn as much as you can about the Internet—it means business. Talk to other artists who use the Internet in their business. Find out what mistakes they've made and successes they've had.

WEB SITES

If you're leery of someone downloading and copying your artwork from your site, then this is not the place for you to exhibit! If your web designer creates the site properly, however, you will have reproductions that are only 72 dots per inch/dpi called jpgs (pronounced jay-pegs). When downloaded, these jpgs do not print very clearly; professional printers usually use 1200 dpi resolution. Using these jpgs for reproduction purposes would not be wise. If a potential hijacker tries to use them, they will print out blurry and not as a final product should.

Reviewing artwork via the Internet has become commonplace in the new millennium for artworld professionals.

➤ Choose an easily understood URL. Match it to your e-mail address as best you can.

➤ Create a simple, easy-to-maneuver web site.

➤ Think how a licensee thinks—in stylistic categories. Divide your web site into stylistic sections: landscapes, abstracts, animals, etc.

➤ Make sure your jpgs do your artwork justice.

➤ Have a link to your e-mail on every page for easy communication.

ON-LINE GALLERIES

You don't have to have your own domain to show your work on the Internet. There are many companies who provide you a homepage where your potential clients can view your artwork.

www.artmarketing.com/gallery
A gallery of 100+ artists with 150,000+ hits per month (and rising!); about 700 people per day browse through this site. ArtNetwork is in contact with publishers, galleries, consultants, designers, licensors, agents as well as other artworld professionals—50,000 annually. Annual fee to exhibit five pieces/$115; two years/$160.

Every artist doing business should have an e-mail address and web site. Don't forget to pick up your messages reglarly. People have come to expect quick responses!

E-MAIL PRESENTATIONS

Licensing agents receive many portfolios each week via e-mail. E-mail presentations can be a very simple way to review, and by far the easiest way to send, a portfolio. A simple e-mail message with four low-resolution images (jpgs) can introduce a publisher to your work without them doing much at all, except opening their e-mail. It's also easy to respond—click "reply" and the publisher can type in a memo and return it to you.

➤ To get their attention on your original e-mail (they receive many from artists and "spammers" daily), be innovative.

➤ Copy and paste your images right within the e-mail.

➤ Include a hyper-link (http://) to your web site address (called a URL), i.e., http://artmarketing.com

CD-ROMS

More and more presentations are being developed in CD-ROM format. Some publishers don't have the facilities to easily review artwork in this medium, however. Before you send a CD-ROM, check with the individual to whom you are mailing to see if she is set up for this kind of presentation.

A CD presentation should consist of a simple grouping of designs. If you have different subject matters, have a short menu at the beginning so the art director can chose only those subjects that interest him.

CD-ROM PRODUCER

Rocket Digital
Mark O'Brien
4141 S Tamiami Trl, Sarasota, FL 34231
941/929-0960
www.rocketdigital.net <mark@rocketdigital.net>
Rocket Digital offers one of the most economical ways to market your work via CD-ROM (it even includes music). They create a fabulous CD-ROM for $250-350. Each CD has a personalized label and can be produced in MAC or PC format. Copies (minimum order 10) are only $2.50 each, including labeling.

Computer screens can only project 72 dpi. Having your images on your site at larger dpi only makes for a longer time to download, possibly irritating potential viewers.

Make sure you put your copyright information on the CD cover as well as within the presentation.

Photojam.pro is a good program to use for making slide shows on CD. It requires Adobe Photoshop as well as an experienced operator to create the slide show.

TELEPHONE CONTACT

Any business requires that you know how to communicate on the phone in a comfortable manner. Don't expect magic from your first contacts—one has to learn how to ask the right questions and say the right things.

Plan your contact times well. Have your questions ready. Be in the right mood to chat. Don't fret about the cost of a call—that should be the least of your concerns!

ASK

➤ What style of work does the company use?

➤ What products does the company produce?

➤ Do they like artwork produced in a certain size?

➤ Do they have a requirement list?

➤ Do they have preferred papers or art boards they wish artists to use?

➤ Do they have specific dates for submissions?

POINTERS

➤ Be nonthreatening.

➤ Don't talk fast.

➤ Keep the pitch of your voice low.

➤ Do not call if you're in a bad mood.

➤ Don't appear overly cheerful.

➤ Qualify the person on the other end: is she the actual person who will be reviewing your work?

➤ Be businesslike and professional—try to sound like you've been doing this for years.

POSSIBLE PHONE DIALOGUE

Hi, my name is .... I am an artist and would like to submit a presentation to the art buyer or art director. Can you tell me their name? Is it possible to put me through to that department?

When you are put through:

Hello, my name is .... I'd like to submit a presentation of my work to you for review. Would you prefer laser copies or can you review a CD presentation or..........?

Ask only a few simple questions if the buyer sounds busy. Respecting her time will get you points.

➤ Are there any particular subjects you are looking for at present?

➤ Do you buy art year-round or do you have specific buying periods?

➤ Do you have a standard fee structure?

➤ What other products do you produce besides............?

FOLLOW-UP

It's amazing to see how many businesspeople (and not only artists) drop the ball at the follow-up juncture. You may figure that since someone didn't call you back, that someone is not interested. Often it means they are just too busy and need you to get on their tails!

Follow-up is a critical step: busy people appreciate it when an artist calls them to follow up. It shows good business sense—and publishers want that in someone they work with. Sure, you will get a "no" quite often, but you will also get your share of "yeses."

➤ Call and ask for the person you've mailed the presentation to.

➤ Find out if he received it and ask for his opinion.

➤ If you find you are getting a negative response, tell the art director you'll be happy to do a speculative commission if he gives you a brief. This creates an opportunity to produce a piece of work to the client's needs and may be a way of proving yourself. It may be that an artwork just doesn't fit the requirements but, with a little art direction, you can produce a piece he would buy.

Working with some licensees in the beginning in this manner can help create a good relationship. In effect, they are helping you produce work that is more sellable for their product range.

TRADE SHOWS

Trade shows are the place to see and be seen.

Trade shows are a major source of research, so don't ignore them when exploring your marketplace. If you live a long distance from New York, where many of the big shows take place, you will also find some in Atlanta, Chicago, Los Angeles, as well as other major cities (see Chapter 10 under "Trade Shows").

THE VISIT

Once you've located a show you think you'd like to visit, call the organizers. If it's early enough (two or three months before the show), ask them to put you on the mailing list for an entry ticket. In some cases entry will be free if you preregister, whereas if you just turn up on the day of the show, you may have to pay a hefty entry fee ($20-50). As these shows are often for the "trade only" (manufacturers, publishers, agents, etc.), don't act like a member of the public when you call. If you have a business name, use that when leaving your address—John Doe Design or Jane Smith Studios. This sounds much more professional and gets you on the mailing list without need for explanation.

Visiting a major trade show such as Surtex or The National Stationery Show, both in New York, can be a daunting task for first-timers.

➤ Allow two days to walk the show.

➤ After registering and getting your catalog of exhibitors, sit down for half an hour or so and go through the catalog.

➤ Identify any companies with whom you'd really like to meet.

➤ Work your way row by row looking for companies who you feel may like your work.

➤ Book your overnight stay well in advance.

➤ Always wear comfortable shoes. You might walk 10-15 miles a day!

➤ Before arriving, try to make an appointment with the art director.

An excellent way to meet people in the industry is to stay at a hotel that the trade show recommends—most of the exhibitors attending will be staying there too. When you ride on the jitney to the show, you will be able to chat with them in an informal manner and learn lots of information.

TIPS

➤ Remember that exhibitors are there to sell their products.

➤ When approaching a booth, ask who the art buyer or art director is. Get a business card. If you are able to talk to him, simply introduce yourself as an artist and ask if you can submit work after the show. You may be lucky and be asked to show some work on the spot. If the buyer is busy, just be happy to get his business card.

➤ Quite often, the person you talk to is a sales rep, i.e., the one who goes on the road selling product. He usually doesn't know the first thing about art, so don't even try to discuss anything with him. Simply ask for the name of the art buyer or creative director, and contact that person after the show.

➤ If you find the buyer friendly, ask a few questions about the range of work he publishes. Is he looking for anything particular at the moment? When are his buying periods? What rights does he normally buy, i.e., US or international?

➤ Have one of your brochures handy so you can leave it. Carry a small portfolio of your work, but it must be simple to review and need little or no explanation.

➤ Try to get to know as much about the company as you can. Get a brochure from them. This will come in handy when you get back to your studio and try to remember who publishes what.

➤ Be methodical when walking a big trade show; otherwise, you might miss that one important company.

➤ Don't be put off if someone is rude. The worst that can happen is that they don't want to look at your work. Move on to the next booth.

➤ If the show has a gala opening event, be sure to attend it. The tickets might cost a bit, but the contacts you make will be worth it. People are much more open and chatty after hours.

At the end of the day you will be tired, and a little bewildered, but you will have met a few dozen potential clients and have lots of business cards. When you return to your studio, you can follow up with mail presentations and phone calls where appropriate.

The publishing/licensing world is very competitive. Timing is of the essence. Publishers need to find the "right" artist before the next publishing house does.

CHAPTER 5

ACTION PLAN

Use the answers to the questions at right to create your action plan.

1.
_____

2.
_____

3.
_____

4.
_____

5.
_____

6.
_____

7.
_____

8.
_____

9.
_____

10.
_____

❑ Compile a database of six potential licensees with contact names and what they each do. Add information as you get it on their fee structure, royalty rates and buying periods.

_____   _____

_____   _____

_____   _____

_____   _____

_____   _____

❑ Prepare a list of trade shows to visit.

_____   _____

_____   _____

❑ Get your name on their mailing list for brochures.

❑ Prepare a leaflet with examples of your work for promotional purposes.

❑ Prepare a portfolio.

❑ Send 20 mailers out each month.

❑ Try to allot a time each day, say an hour, or at least twice a week, to make follow-up calls.

❑ Visit several new web sites each week to see what's happening. You can visit art galleries' sites, art publishers, greeting card and stationery companies. Just type in a product or a subject at a search engine and surf around.

Chapter 6
Licensing Agents

What is an agent?

The interview

Fee structures

Locating an agent

Overseas markets

I shut my eyes in order to see.

Paul Gauguin

WHAT IS AN AGENT?

Having an agent frees you up to concentrate on what you do best—produce new art.

A licensing agent is a matchmaker between an artist's work and an appropriate licensee (publisher or product manufacturer). She negotiates business arrangements and legal contracts in relationship to licensing and publishing for the artist. A licensing agent is always looking for the perfect "marriage" in the marketplace for the artist and product.

Getting an agent takes time, effort (attending a licensing show, calling agents), money (buying a directory) and also the appropriate art for a particular niche market.

Agents often work with a specific product line or property sector (see "Property Sectors," page 19), i.e., some only work with celebrities or entertainment properties, some only with art and design. Having an agent is well worth the commission you pay. Agents are more aware of the marketplace, thus able to get more licenses. Being your own agent in this field is a full-time job that you may not want.

Choosing an agent is not difficult if you follow some simple rules. Using the reference section in the second half of this book, you will find a list of agents. The entries will help you distinguish what topics, styles and genres each company specializes in.

FINDING AN AGENT

Once you have selected those who handle the style of work you produce, call to find out their submission procedures. (In some cases they are listed in this book.) Be sure to follow any procedure they request.

Make life easy for the agent. The agency you will be dealing with may have several staff members, each dealing with certain types of artwork. Until they actually see what style you produce, they may not know who you will be working with. Only a certain amount of time is dedicated to meeting with artists—those artists who the agent feels have the quality and standard of work, as well as subject matter and style that he can sell.

A good agent tries to develop a comprehensive line of products that can be merchandised.

Agents receive many submissions a week and may already have artists they work with who have a similar style to your own. If that's the case, they might not want two artists of the same style competing within their company, even though your work is good.

FACTORS AGENTS ARE LOOKING FOR IN AN ARTIST

➤ Is your work commercial and saleable?

➤ Are you easy to work with?

➤ Can you meet deadlines?

➤ Are you reliable?

➤ Can you execute a specific design request?

➤ Is the standard of your work consistent?

➤ Are you easy to contact?

➤ Do you specialize only or are you flexible and versatile?

ADVANTAGES OF HAVING AN AGENT

➤ An agent has far greater expertise and experience in the industry than most artists.

➤ An agent has many connections with licensees. As an artist, if you are with a good agent, you stand a far better chance of having your work seen by manufacturers.

➤ Agents are likely to get higher fees for you. They understand what value the art has to the licensee. They are often more skilled in negotiating.

➤ Agents can help you fine-tune your projects and offer art direction and ideas to pursue.

It is quite possible to have more than one agent. If one agent, for instance, specializes only in fine art prints, limited editions and posters, it leaves you free to have an agent for stationery, greeting cards and gift products.

Agents vary considerably from one-person companies to small businesses with up to half a dozen staff, to large companies who have overseas connections handling art and design, entertainment properties and brand licensing.

Choose an agent who has experience in the product you feel your art will work well with, and who has been in business a few years so that s/he already has a good number of licensees as clients.

Fine art publishers often act as agents for their artists, showcasing their work at licensing shows.

An agent has spent many years nurturing his licensees. The last thing he wants to happen is to let a licensee down by late arrival of artwork or substandard work.

THE INTERVIEW

Interviewing with an agent can be daunting. Being nervous is not unusual. It is important you make a good impression; after all, agents can make an artist's career through their contacts and knowledge. Don't be hesitant to ask questions about how the agent operates. In fact, a good agent will appreciate that you are concerned about your career.

QUESTIONS TO ASK

➤ What are their commission rates?

➤ What are their major markets?

➤ At what trade shows do they attend or exhibit?

➤ Ask to review their agency agreement.

➤ Ask to review their standard licensing agreement.

➤ Ask for references from their client list.

YOUR PRESENTATION

In a portfolio, the agent is looking for talent, creativity and quality. Be very discerning and specific in what you show in your portfolio.

The idea is to "knock him out" with your portfolio so he really wants to sign you up. Make your portfolio impressive. (See *Art Marketing 101* for details on how to develop a portfolio.) Make it unique, a specific style, and easy to review.

➤ When you meet, hand the portfolio to the agent and allow her to go through it at her own pace. Often, artists want to explain each image in detail. This is totally unnecessary. Only answer questions.

➤ Show your very best work—no mediocre pieces.

➤ Leave out material that doesn't relate to the commercial market.

Each agent's terms will vary considerably. Following are some guidelines as to the kinds of arrangements that can be agreed upon.

➤ Agents' fees vary from 25% to as much as 75% of your part of the royalty. The norm, and a fair rate, is around 35 - 50%.

➤ Some agents may charge extra on overseas work (60%), especially if they are making overseas telephone calls and shipping work abroad. Although this may appear high, think of what it would cost you to set up deals with overseas manufacturers in Europe, Australia or Japan! Usually, sales overseas are over and above licensing deals in the USA, so be happy with your 40%.

FEE STRUCTURES

COMMISSIONS

If you are lucky enough to be taken on by a reputable agency, ensure that whenever you take on a commission you:

➤ Understand the intent of the commission fully.

➤ Accept the deadline for sketches.

➤ Deliver the artwork on time, every time.

EXCLUSIVITY

Exclusivity is very important. It is not good for an agent building up a healthy licensing program and new commissions to discover you're too busy doing jobs for other people.

You also need to be careful, however, with the idea of exclusivity. If you want to do book jackets or book illustrations and the agent doesn't work in that field, then exclude book illustration from your contract. You can then work with another agent in this other field.

If you want to generate a good income from licensing, agents are the best path. They can accomplish more in a shorter period of time—that's their business.

THE IMPORTANCE OF BEING TIMELY

I got a call on a Friday afternoon from the art director of a major licensee who wanted 200 designs for greeting cards in four weeks—an almost impossible task. We acted without delay. All the commission agreements were sent out in writing to the artists, along with a phone call to explain what was required. Sketches were required within three to four days. Then, on approval, the artists had approximately three weeks to complete up to six pieces of artwork.

The deadline arrived. One artist's work was missing. An urgent phone call was placed to chase down the artwork. When found, the artist quite calmly told us that he'd finished three pieces but hadn't been able to finish the rest—his family had turned up unexpectedly and he just hadn't had time.

You can imagine my reaction knowing that the publisher's printer was waiting to print a sheet of 16 designs with three designs missing. The repercussions were enormous.

Not only had the printer's time been prearranged to print, but the printer also had to proof, print, cut, trim, film wrap, box and deliver each design (5000 cards of each) by a specific date.

A delay like this can cost thousands of dollars. Retail groups have specific buying periods and delivery dates so that they can get the cards into their selling system, sales conferences and product catalogs. Can you imagine the chaos that can be caused by a delay of this kind? The artist is just a few days late in his mind, while the art director and printer are thinking about throwing themselves off the nearest skyscraper!

The repercussions of not delivering artwork on time can be disastrous. Avoid delays at all costs. If you are ill or for some reason are unavoidably delayed, let the agent know as soon as you think there could be a problem. Don't wait until the last minute.

Another example is a delay on a finished piece of art for a collector plate. In this instance, the manufacturer had booked space in one of the Sunday magazines at a cost of around $15,000. This was to be a test ad showing a new plate design.

You can imagine the manufacturer's response when the art for the plate wasn't ready. Not only did they lose the space, but the ad was then delayed for months until another suitable slot and date could be arranged.

Quite often, ads are chosen to appear at specific times, avoiding certain days or weeks due to holidays, major events, etc. These dates are specific and important. Missing a certain time slot could delay a project by weeks or even months.

Very rarely do artists realize the full implications of delays. Miss an important deadline at your own peril. Not only does the agent lose confidence in you, but the licensee can lose confidence in the agent. A major loss of faith by a manufacturer could mean thousands of dollars of lost business for you.

BOOKS

Licensing Art 101
The book you are holding in your hand has lists of agents in Chapter 10.

The Artists and Graphic Designers Market
F&W Publications
4700 E Galbraith Rd Cincinnati, OH 45236
800/289-0963 513/531-2222

Writers' & Artists' Yearbook
A&C Black
Linda Lambert
37 Soho Sq, London W1D 3QZ England
0207/758-0200
www.acblack.com <wayb@acblack.com>
A must if you want to find clients or an agent in England. It has a list of greeting card manufacturers, newspapers, magazines and children's book publishers. Approximately $18.

Licensing Resource Directory: The Who's Who of the Licensing Industry
International Licensing Industry Merchanders' Association/LIMA
350 Fifth Ave #1408, New York, NY 10018-0110
212/244-1944
www.licensing.org <info@licensing.org>
This is the main licensing organization in the world. They have a very useful web site that lists information about the licensing industry as well as agents. Membership starts at $500 per year.

DIRECTORY

ArtFolio
ArtNetwork
PO Box 1360, Nevada City, CA 95959-1360
800/383-0677 530/470-0862
www.artmarketing.com/artfolio <info@artmarketing.com>
This directory of 98 artists is sent out to over 4000 publishers (greeting card, calendar, book and art) and licensing agents. Interested professionals call upon the artists directly from their listing in the directory. It is published biannually in even-numbered years. Advertising costs $499 for a full page. Artists are juried into the book. Call for a brochure.

LOCATING AN AGENT

Agents often have booths at trade shows. See the list of trade shows in the resource section of this book.

OVERSEAS MARKETS

If your agent's standard commission is 50%, then on a $1000 deal generated by the Japanese agent, your own agent will receive $600 net and you will receive $300— 50%.

The UK is by far the easiest foreign market for American artists to approach; however, you need to know whether your style of artwork will sell in the UK. If it's too "American," it may not work, just as some "English" designs don't work over here.

You may have a style of artwork with potential in Europe, or Japan or Australia. It is possible to enlist the services of an agent in a particular country.

The simplest way to deal with the overseas marketplace is to let your US agent handle those sales, working directly or through foreign agents. While you will be paying two commissions if deals come through another agent, the hassle of dealing with it yourself could be far more costly in time and money. The US agent might, for instance, have arrangements with a Japanese agent who will work on a 40% commission on any sales he produces. The Japanese agent will remit what is due to your US agent, who will normally charge his usual commission rate just as he would for a US publisher. He still has to send the work out to the foreign country, as well as negotiate the fee and do all the usual paperwork. This can be more costly to administer than a sale in the US.

This is an effective way of generating good sales overseas. Also, your agent will have had to find a reliable agent in the foreign country, and while far from infallible, agents are usually astute businesspeople who will have vetted the agent carefully, or even visited him.

If you do, however, decide to work directly with overseas agents, then attend Licensing International in New York in June. It is the best place to find direct representation. A number of UK and European agents have booths there.

You might attend trade shows such as the National Stationery Show or ArtExpo, both in New York, to find agents. Major foreign companies often have a sales office in the US.

Only approach major international foreign publishers: they will speak English well and will be used to dealing with artists in different countries. Working with the smaller companies can be problematic due to language difficulties. If you do have a problem with the smaller company, it can be difficult to resolve from 4000 miles away.

Delayed payments, lack of information and bad communication are common problems. These will be avoided by having a US agent deal with a foreign agent or licensee.

Compile a list of 12 potential agents to call.

_____

_____

_____

_____

_____

_____

_____

_____

Prepare a list of trade shows to visit.

_____

_____

_____

_____

❏ Research agents' web sites to see what's happening.

ACTION PLAN

Use the answers to the questions at left to create your action plan.

1. _____

2. _____

3. _____

4. _____

5. _____

6. _____

7. _____

8. _____

9. _____

10. _____

Chapter 7
Self-Publishing Prints

Advantages and disadvantages

Limited editions

Giclées

Giclée service bureaus

Promotion

Success is what sells.
Andy Warhol

ADVANTAGES AND DISADVANTAGES

There are two basic methods of getting your work into print:

➤ Having an established art publisher print and market: you receive a royalty, as explained in the previous chapters.

➤ Publishing it yourself: you pay for printing and you market the printed pieces yourself.

If you are having no luck finding a publisher, self-publishing can be a way to start. In the long run, however, a good publisher has developed a consumer base through a large distribution channel. Thus, he can afford to advertise nationally and produce glossy catalogs and attend the major trade shows.

Self-publishing is not something you should consider lightly. You need three to four years of hard work to stand any chance of achieving regular sales figures. It can take several years to build up a good collector base. Many artists make the mistake of jumping into self-publishing and forget about the marketing aspects.

For some artists, self-publishing is the right direction to go. If you already have outlets at which to sell prints—outdoor shows, galleries in which your originals hang, tourist shops, etc.—then the marketing has already been set in motion to some extent.

ADVANTAGES OF SELF-PUBLISHING

➤ You have total control of the production of your image.

➤ If you sell at outdoor shows, self-publishing can be a boost to your sales.

➤ You increase exposure to other economic levels that can't be reached with originals.

➤ If your prints begin selling, your originals can become even more valuable.

➤ People who like your work and originally buy a $100 print will often return as collectors and buy another print or an original.

The key to self-publishing is to start small and build up distribution gradually.

DISADVANTAGES OF SELF-PUBLISHING

➤ Output of money for prints and marketing

➤ Output of time: you must do all the research, marketing, etc. You might be able to locate a distributor, but this also takes time and searching.

➤ You personally have to sell 50 times the quantity of an original (if you print limited editions of 50). How many originals have you sold?

➤ Your competitors are established publishers who have distribution channels built up over many years, as well as other artists.

RESEARCH

You'll need to start your marketing by doing lots of research: become familiar with the current print market; go to print and poster galleries, ask them what sells. Get brochures from big publishing houses; look at magazines to see what is advertised and what is selling. This research is not dissimilar to the research you may have done to locate appropriate publishers.

Spend some focused time thinking about the marketing of your prints before you actually commit to printing. You need to have a detailed marketing plan in position before you spend money on giclées or any other form of printing. If you have been refused over and over again by publishers in the business, have you asked them why?

Fashions and tastes can be fickle. Many popular prints are plagiarized remorselessly to the extent that a top-selling style is often emulated by several publishers who get their artists to produce similar versions. These versions do not necessarily infringe copyright, but they look similar enough to the uneducated eye. This often has the effect of killing off a particular popular style sooner than the original publisher of the art would want.

Become familiar with the four-color printing process. Some colors in your original artwork may be difficult to reproduce, i.e., flourescent, oranges, some teals and purples, reds.

LIMITED EDITIONS

Personalize it: sign it, repaint on it, frame it uniquely.

Don't even think about producing open-edition prints (i.e., editions with no limit). The prices of open editions at wholesale can be so low that you would have to sell 10,000 prints or more to have any success. Leave this to the big publishers who have established large distribution.

Limited editions vary from around 95 to 950 for the big publishers. For you, an individual artist, a first-time limited should have a run of 25-95. If you sell out within one or two years or less, great! Your new work can be published in a higher-numbered limited edition, say 95-195. Slowly increase your runs. You want to set about creating a collectors' market.

➤ When you produce a limited-edition print, you must keep track of *each* print that is taken out of the studio, whether on consignment, to be framed, sold (note the collector's name and how much she paid), or for an exhibit. Use your job cards to keep track of this.

➤ The market for a limited-edition print is regulated by law in a number of states, including California, Illinois and New York. Extensive disclosures or disclaimers may have to accompany limited-edition prints sold in these states, verifying print run, etc.

CREATING A COLLECTORS' MARKET

The whole point of selling limited-edition prints is to create a collector base, i.e., buyers who love to collect your work. By having small editions, you stand a greater chance of selling out of a particular edition, which is exactly what you want to occur. To be able to say "sold out" is great. This is what creates demand, eventually raising prices of both originals and prints. Collectors who love collecting don't want to miss out on your next edition.

Top publishers love this to happen to their artists, as it creates a secondary market where galleries sometimes buy back prints to satisfy important collectors who are willing to pay a lot more just to get a copy of a print they've missed. Some "sold out" editions from big names can fetch thousands of dollars.

➤ The key is to emulate what the top publishers do but on a smaller scale, keeping the editions small, of high quality and reasonably priced.

➤ It's a no-no to produce an open-edition print and a limited-edition print of the same artwork.

When you mail postcards to your collectors about your newest edition, it's important to emphasize to them to "'buy now to avoid missing this edition."

TIPS

➤ Take photos of several pieces you will be printing to frame shops in your area. Ask the owners which pieces they like the best. Print from the results of your research. Go back to these same shops and sell the prints.

➤ Do a test by making a photo print of your piece; mat it and take it to your next art show. Find out what price you can ask and what quantity you can sell. Is anyone nibbling? What size would sell best for you? If you decide to do a limited edition of this test piece, do not sell this open-edition piece! Discard it.

➤ You need to know your printing costs (get quotes from several printers), who your target market is, and the number of prints you must sell to break even.

➤ Make contacts with distributors, approach possible free promotional sources and design your marketing materials.

➤ Go door-to-door to stores, galleries, restaurants and businesses.

➤ Perhaps you can get financing from former buyers or collectors by offering them the first print in the series. You'll be gathering the necessary money and selling prints at the same time.

➤ Some printers use coatings to protect the finished work. You'll need to familiarize yourself with types of coatings.

➤ Create a certificate of authenticity that states (page 97 in *Art Marketing 101*) how many prints you've published.

Compose a brochure with all the prints you publish in it—put "sold out" next to those that are no longer available.

GICLÉES

Giclée means 'ink spray' in French.

Stockpiling an inventory of prints is no longer necessary. The newest method of printing that has enabled many artists to self-publish, due to its affordability, is the giclée print.

The original giclées were produced by an Iris printer, which was, in fact, used as a proofing machine. It was due to the foresight of rock musician Graham Nash and a colleague that this technology was then developed to produce artists' prints. Companies such as Epson, Roland, Hewlett-Packard and Colorspan are all producing inkjet (giclée) machines. There are, in fact, so many machines of varying quality that it is impossible to cover all the processes in any depth.

The Iris Graphics Printer was first presented at a trade show in 1987. Designed for color accuracy, it did not at that time find its way into the fine-art market, mostly due to the lack of archival longevity. Through the years the archival quality has improved. Since 1994, Iris printers have been on the market for fine-art reproductions. The Iris printer is a four-color, continuous-tone printer that can accurately reproduce multiple color transitions and intricate detail. Print quality is as good as, and some say better than, screen printing or traditional lithography. Iris printers create images by spraying microscopic droplets from a nozzle onto a substrate that is attached to a drum. These droplets, indistinguishable to the naked eye, build a lush and vivid surface at 1200-1800 dpi, making this method of reproduction quite good for hard-edged painting or fine-grained photographs.

PRINTNG STEPS

Copy shot - Photographing the artwork to reproduce in a large format, usually as a scan or transparency

Digital file - Time invested in reworking a good digital file will influence the printing of the image forever. The artist will have the option of experimenting with many different controls offered by the computer process. When a digital version is finalized, printing begins.

Media - Paper and canvas are the most common media. You'll need to become knowledgeable about the many paper choices available.

Inks - Archival inks are a must.

Printing - This should be a collaborative process involving the artist and printer. A proof is made for the artist's approval.

You need to remember that different batches of inks create slightly different tones.

Finishing - Trimming, cutting, hand-torn edges and coatings are some options.

Archiving - Saving your final computer digital file for future printing (you are only printing part of your limited-edition run at any given time). This will be done by the service bureau.

Shipping - Tubes and boards are needed for secure shipping.

Reordering - When you need additional prints, you can order from your giclée service bureau by fax or telephone.

WORKING WITH A GICLÉE SERVICE BUREAU

➤ Each service bureau prices and works differently with its artists.

➤ Get a quote in writing so there is no confusion in the future.

➤ You might want to have the printer add to his quote, "No additional images are printed for any reason whatsoever without the explicit written permission of the artist."

➤ It is good to have a "Note of Verification," which states, "I guarantee that the above information is correct and that no other proofs or impressions exist that are not part of this documentation sheet." This should be signed by both printer and artist.

➤ Documenting these prints is important. Note artist, title of work, medium, image size, paper size, paper type, print run, edition size, number of proofs and pertinent dates.

There are also opportunities to add value to giclées by "remarquing"—a process reserved essentially for higher-quality giclées, wherby the artist can work on the actual print with paint or other media to enhance the print and its value, making it an "original."

A GICLÉE PRIMER

BY KATE DARDINE

You've seen them at shows and galleries. You've heard people talking about them. You've read articles about collectors snapping them up. Every art magazine runs ads for them. So now, you are ready to take the leap and have your artwork reproduced as a giclée.

NOT ALL GICLÉES ARE CREATED EQUAL

Some printers use archival pigmented inks, some use dye-based inks with a wide color range but shorter life span. Some printers have no apparent "digital signature" (posterization, pixelization, dot pattern, etc.); others leave a distinctive dot pattern. Which printer model you choose depends on which factors are most important to you as an artist—color accuracy, ability to capture subtle gradations in color/tone, choice of papers, maximum size, price. Once you've prioritized your needs, you can then begin to look for a service bureau whose equipment and expertise best matches your needs.

QUALITY OF IMAGE

Scanners determine a good portion of the printing quality. Start with a premium scan and you're in for fewer problems.

IMAGE STABILITY

How long will a print last before noticeably fading? Both ink and paper must be considered. Some desktop printer inks only last two years, others claim to last 100. Most inks used by fine art printers last a minimum of 15 years, some last 70, and some pigmented inks last over 100. It is the combination of ink and paper that determines archival qualities. How the print is stored and displayed also affects image stability. To insure that your print will last as long as possible, inform your purchasers how to care for it.

SIZES AVAILABLE

Small prints (up to 13x44") can be printed on an office printer (Epson Stylus Pro 5500) with the help of PhotoShop. For larger sizes, you will need an established giclée service bureau with an Iris or other large-format printer.

PRICE

Some fine art printers charge per square inch, some per sheet. Some charge a higher setup fee with lower print prices, some the opposite. Most end up falling into a similar price range. If you find a bargain-price printer, chances are your prints will be bargain-price quality.

PAPER

Choice of paper or canvas is a decision that should be based on the artist's preference, the artwork to be reproduced and the market where the giclée will be sold.

You need personal guidance and assistance from experienced staff when deciding how to print your giclées. Once you have found a service bureau whose equipment matches your needs and whose technicians are knowledgeable and skilled, you are most of the way to getting the best-quality print.

The quality of anything you sell will determine repeat customers—clients telling their friends about your product. If you're going to do a giclée, do it right. Make a statement. Sell for a lifetime.

Kate is a customer relations specialist at Fine Print Imaging, a giclée printer located. She welcomes questions about printing and marketing fine art reproductions. Contact her at 1306 Blue Spruce Dr, Fort Collins, CO 80524-2067 800/777-1141 970/484-9650 970/416-6352 Fax www.fineprintimaging.com <kdardine@fineprintimaging.com>

GICLÉE SERVICE BUREAUS

Blazing Editions
PO Box 1954, East Greenwich, RI 02818 401/885-4329
www.blazing.com

Canvas Imaging
118 E 59th St, New York, NY 10022 212/980-2984

Classic Editions
3185-G Airway Ave, Costa Mesa, CA 92626 714/432-7212
www.ClassicEditions.com <info@classiceditions.com>

ColorSpan
7850 Shady Oak Rd, Eden Prairie, MN 55344-0858 800/390-8616
www.colorspan.com

Cook Editions
1740 DeFoor Pl, Atlanta, GA 30318 404/351-6776

Coupralux Fine Art Printmaking and Gallery
1616C Hi Line Dr, Dallas, TX 75207 800/270-4177
www.coupralux.com <bowers@coupralux.com>

Finer Image Editions
5901 Noble Ave, Van Nuys, CA 91411 800/464-2864 818/373-1100
www.finerimage.com <FinerImage@linkline.com>

Fine Print Imaging
1306 Blue Spruce Dr, Fort Collins, CO 80524-2067
(800) 777 1141 (970) 484 9650 (970) 416 6352 Fax
 www.fineprintimaging.com <kdardine@fineprintimaging.com>

Harvest Productions
8050 E Crystal Dr, Anaheim, CA 92807-2524 714/279-2300

Hunter Editions
PO Box 1130, Kennebunkport, ME 04046 888/278-4747
www.huntereditions.com

Old Town Editions
205 S Union St, Alexandria, VA 22314 703/684-0005
www.oldtowneditions.com

One World Art Printing
2070 Hwy 89A, Sedona, AZ 86336 877/PRINT-ART
www.oneworldart.com

Real Color
Mary Anne Belle
556 Ocean View, santa Cruz, CA 95062
831/457-0115
www.santacruzdigitalarts.org

SMP Digital Graphics
15 W 20th St, New York, NY 10011 212/691-6766
www.smpdigital.com

Sutton Graphics
9 Niagara St, Toronto, Ontario M5V 1C2 Canada 416/598-4031

Talon Graphics
1021 Calle Sombra #B, San Clemente, CA 92673

Triumphant Printers
111 Watkins Ave, Oneonta, NY 13820
607/674-5666
www.studiogiclee.com <vze2n29@verizon.net>

Winthrop Editions
49 Central St, West Boylston, MA   508/835-4880
www.winthropeditions.com <ngallery@tiac.net>

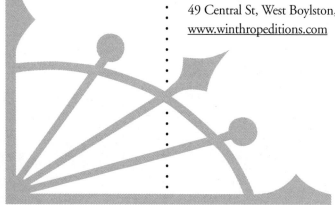

A typical cost for producing the first of a series of giclée ranges from $170-350 (20x40" image) on watercolor paper with UV coating. Subsequent reorders will cost less. Ten prints will cost an average of $60 each.

PRICING FOR PROFIT

➤ There should be some relationship between the cost of your originals and the cost of your prints. Limited-edition giclée prints generally run between 5-20% of your original prices.

➤ The retail price should be at least five times your actual cost. When calculating the cost, figure out the entire run's cost.

Example

The first print costs $300, which includes the pre-print costs of scanning, etc. The next 49 prints each cost $60. Total for all 50 prints will be $3240. Divided by $50, this brings the cost of each to $65. Five times the cost of $65 is $325.

Are your originals selling for $3250 (10%)? If your originals are selling for $1900, can you sell this print for $325 (about 17%)? Perhaps if it is large enough, there will be no problem. If your work is selling for $1500, $330 is probably too much. No one will buy. Your print price should be more like $150. You could make your print edition larger (but perhaps never sell out) or lower your price and not wholesale your pieces. As your original work rises in price, there is more likelihood a buyer will pay $330 for a limited-edition piece of 50.

Ultimately, you can sell your prints for whatever you like. You want to make a profit in line with work of equal quality and value.

There are giclée prints that can be produced for less that $60 using less expensive equipment. Always check the image stability and always use archival inks.

If your originals are selling for just a few hundred dollars, then retail prices of $325 for a giclée will be too high. However, it is important to retain a pricing policy of four times markup as an absolute minimum if you want to sell to galleries at wholesale. if you simply double the cost of the print, you could not afford to sell at 50% discount to a gallery.

SHIPPING SUPPLIES

MasterPak
145 E 57th St, New York, NY 10022-2141
800/922-5522 212/765-7056
www.masterpak-usa.com
Call for their detailed borchure on all their packaging products.

COSTS

The beauty of printing a giclée is that you don't have the huge up-front costs nor storage problems associated with litho editions—you can print small quantities or just one at a time, called "on-demand printing."

TRADE SHOWS

The first three years an artist displays at a trade show can be the toughest ones. The distributors are checking artists out for the first three years. They want to make sure the artist comes back and is still producing quality work.

TIPS

➤ Hire a rep to assist with your first trade show. A rep can show you the ropes and introduce you to distributors.

➤ Prepare a written list of details for getting ready to go to the show. Follow it!

➤ Prepay for electrical hookup, table rentals, etc.—it wil cost twice as much after the show starts.

➤ Make hotel reservations well in advance. Stay in the hotel where the show has its headquarters so as not to miss out on networking opportunities.

➤ Set up the day before the show starts.

➤ Smaller shows seem to attract local frame shops and galleries that are looking for new work. They tend to buy on the spot.

➤ Start with local shows, then expand to the big one in Atlanta—the National Showcase.

PRINT TRADE SHOW

Art Buyers Caravan
330 N 4th St, St Louis, MO 63102 314/421-5445
Shows throughout the country sponsored by Decor *magazine. They also publish* Decor Magazine Sources; *their annual issue that comes out in May.*

PROMOTION

So you've begun printing limited editions, you have sold only a couple and you need to expand your market.

➤ If you have galleries selling your originals, they might want to have a different price point to sell.

➤ If you have a private exhibit, or if you do outdoor shows, this is the perfect place to sell limited editions.

➤ Local galleries or specialty shops are your next best bet.

ADVERTISING AND PUBLICITY

An artist from Northern California stated that the most important aspect of selling prints is getting your name out there.

➤ Create a distinctive advertising campaign and logo design so people will remember you.

➤ Plan a good publicity schedule.

➤ If you advertise, be sure to do repeat advertising. Your image and logo must be repeated over and over.

Advertising is expensive. If you have a specialized subject such as marine, trains, wildlife, equine, etc., then advertising in a specific genre magazine might pay off.

Where possible, try to get publicity/PR. Compose a good press release with a reproduction of your print. Magazines might feature your piece free of charge in their editorial section. Though it can take a lot of legwork and persistence, it's much less expensive than advertising. It also warrants much more interest than an ad.

➤ Send press releases to local newspapers.

➤ Try to get an article by presenting a complete story to an editor (they love that), be persistent with phone calls (but not pesty) and you could become famous locally!

TIP

➤ Local advertising is probably the best place to start. Most towns have a tourist or shopping guide that usually includes a gallery section. Try offering the use of your latest artwork on the cover of the magazine—great publicity. Be sure they give you proper credit, i.e., your name, phone number, web site and e-mail.

➤ Check with y our local Chamber of Commerce. They usually publish a business and tourist guide annually.

ADVERTISING VENUES

Not only are these advertising venues but magazines you need to read to get to know the print business.

Art Business News Annual Guide
800/598-6008
You get this guide when you are a subscriber to Art Business News.

Art Trends
225 Gordons Corner Rd, Manapalan, NJ 07726
800/969-7176
www.arttrends.com

Art World News
887 E Wilmette Rd #C-2, Palatine, IL 60067
847/705-6519
www.artworldnews.com   <jbmale@aol.com>

Giclée Today Magazine
Patrick Sarver
PO Box 420, Manalapan, NJ 07726-0420
732/446-4900
www.gicleestoday.com   <hobbypub@injersey.com>

RESOURCE

ArtNetwork
800/383-0677
Has a mailing list of print distributors—sales reps selling prints wholesale to poster and frame galleries, specialty shops such as zoos, florists, etc.

PUBLICITY VENUE

Showcase

330 N 4th St, St Louis, MO 63102 314/421-5445

Each month Decor *magazine presents new limited editions and posters. Send a press release and photo/slide of any new print. Be sure to include the title, original medium, edition size, quantity of signed and numbered copies, phone number, address, web site and e-mail.*

US Art

220 S Sixth St #500, Minneapolis, MN 55402-4507

800/788-0204 ext 216   612/336-9226

www.mspcommunications.com/pubs/usart

<tmccormick@mspcommunications.com>

"Premieres" is the section of the magazine where new prints are promoted. Submit ifnormation your your new release, as well as a slide, transparency, or digital image.

BOOK

Producing and Marketing Prints

Sue Viders, 9739 Tall Grass Cir, Lone Tree, CO 80124 800/999-7013

www.sueviders.com   <viders@worldnet.att.net>

A great book that takes you through all the steps of self-publishing. $14.95 plus shipping. Also available is an audiotape covering color theory and pricing called Hints on Prints. *The $19.95 price includes a resource booklet.*

WEB SITES

www.studiogiclee.com

Info on the process, papers, inks, etc., as well as prices. This company uses a Colorspan printer, which is at the top end in terms of quality.

www.wilhelm-research.com

Technical information about different machines and inks

ACTION PLAN

Use the answers to the questions at right to create your action plan.

1. _____

2. _____

3. _____

4. _____

5. _____

6. _____

7. _____

8. _____

9. _____

10. _____

❑ Do market research for creating a limited edition.

❑ Calculate the cost of printing these giclées.

First print and pre-press:

Next 49 prints, if printed 4 at a time @ _____

Price of each print = _____

_____

❑ Calculate the price at which you will retail these pieces.

5-10% of original = _____

5 x cost of print =

List your retail buyers:

_____

_____

_____

List your wholesale buyers:

_____

_____

_____

List PR possibilities:

_____

_____

_____

List advertising venues:

_____

_____

_____

Chapter 8

Self-Publishing Cards

Greeting card market

Handmade cards

The printing process

They gave it to me for an un-birthday present.
Through the Looking Glass, *Lewis Carroll*

GREETING CARD MARKET

Reproduction of original art into note cards offers artists the opportunity to participate in a $6 billion market. Of course, the bulk of this market is captured by the very large card companies, but an estimated $1 billion is left to individual artists.

Greeting cards have many uses for artists. Besides the added sales at your shows, they can provide an excellent self-promotion tool: announcing shows, advertising for commissions and introducing new work, either originals or prints.

Depending on your style of art, consider direct sales to historical and tourist attractions, and for fundraising ideas for churches, civic organizations, nonprofits and school groups.

Think of a *new idea* to bring to the greeting card industry. One lady makes cards with buttons attached. Another artist makes fragrant cards, another Braille cards. What is your niche?

Each line, however popular it may be, will need to continue to add new designs and concepts. Once you start a line, you want to expand it by creating cards for a variety of occasions and seasons so both your rep and store remain happy. No one-year marketing plans here! You will need a well-created, five-year business plan to succeed.

CYCLE/TIME-LINE

Often a card has only an eight-month life span, a life span similar to products in the fashion industry. Of course, there are exceptions. Some cards and designs, especially those with well-known characters, will be seen year after year.

The wholesale greeting-card industry has a high and low season. The quieter wholsaling seasons are November-February, when all the Christmas orders have been taken, and indeed the Valentine orders, too. New lines are being prepared for the Spring Stationery Show in New York in mid-May.

TIPS

➤ Cards are put on shelves with the top one-third showing. Create your design and wordage with this in mind.

➤ Cards on uncoated stock are often avoided by store buyers because they become dirty and crumpled from handling.

➤ Most buyers want cards to state the occasion on them, so make your cards specific. Probably 50% of the market is birthday cards; the next largest market is Christmas cards (partly because they're purchased by the box); then Valentine's Day, Easter, Mother's Day, Father's Day, Graduation, Thanksgiving, Halloween.

➤ Make your card appeal to both sexes. If you have to create for one sex, keep in mind that 85-90% of all cards are purchased by women.

➤ Front color is very important.

➤ Colored envelopes can be catchy but not too dark—the writing won't be legible.

➤ Organize your card inventory so you can keep records easily. Each style will probably have a set of 12-16 cards. For coding, put the style, name, and year it was printed on the back as part of your code.

➤ The back of the card should have the name of your card line, logo, artist's name, identification number (you make this up!), price, ™ sign if you've trademarked your image, copyright year, and "Printed in (country)" if imported.

MOCK-UPS

One surefire way to gauge whether you've got a potential winning range of cards is to produce a range of mock-up cards. Use the standard format of 5x7". You can also use this to show to potential publishers. You can show them to friends, family. Keep in mind that this can be misleading: many friends don't want to upset you so they always say they're cute or lovely. Whatever testing you do, unless it's full-scale market research, is at best an educated guess. Many artists simply put them on display at their own art shows around the country.

Follow the industry and attend the best trade show to allow your product to be seen by as many of the retail outlets as possible in the US. By far the best greeting card venue is the Naitonal Stationery Show in New York in May each year. If you can get a booth, no matter how small, the minimum cost is going to be $2500-3000.

CHAPTER 8

COSTS

Mary Englebreit has a great article on her site about getting started in the card industry. www.maryenglebreit.com

Let's say you print 24 designs—any fewer is not really viable.

You sell 1000 of each of the 24 designs at 75¢ wholesale: $18,000. (They are usually sold in groups of 10.) After printing costs, envelopes, a leaflet or brochure, exhibit costs totalling $9000, you will be left with $9000 gross profit. The $9000 covers your time, as well as the basic overhead costs—heat, light, telephone, gas, etc. You can see that you have to sell a lot more than 24,000 cards to make a good profit.

On the other hand, if you sell an average of 3000 of each design—$54,000 gross revenue—with overheads of around $22,500, the figures look a little more appealing.

If you have a range of 48 designs the potential increases, but so do your outlay and risk. You can't really survive on one show per year unless you are prepared to visit lots of customers. You can try to get sales reps throughout the country. This is not easy and you'll have to pay a commission of 10-20%.

PRICING

Greeting cards are sold wholesale by the dozen. For instance, a card that you want to retail at $2.50 will sell wholesale for $15 per dozen (12 x $1.25). Your rep would get 20% or $3 per dozen. (Handmade cards, which can run from $3-10 retail, are sometimes sold individually rather than by the dozen.) $100 is generally the minimum order (i.e., 7 designs x $15 per dozen = $105). Stores don't want to order less than $100 as it's too much trouble. Stores pay the shipping costs.

"Guaranteed Sales" is a term, if in your contract, which will enable a retailer to return goods unsold after a pre-specified time. You don't want this! Soil, tears and marks will make your cards unusable after they are returned. Only large companies can deal with the cost of returns, so don't agree to guaranteed sales under any circumstances. Guaranteed sales is similar to consignment, and you don't want that, either. Consignment is unheard of in the greeting card industry, so don't even offer it to local stores if you are doing the selling yourself.

PRINTING

A large part of your business cost will be the cost of merchandise.

Always get quotes from several different printers. You'll be amazed at the variations in prices among printers. Different presses have different limitations, so the quotes you receive can vary as much as 100%.

Get to know the printer. Get samples of his previous work. Ask for and call to verify referrals. Have questions ready when you call the referrals: Did the printer meet your deadline? Did he have any hidden costs? Did he answer questions promptly during the printing process?

CARD PRINTERS

Color Q
2710 Dryden Rd, Dayton, OH 45439
800/999-1007

Printing Department
2600 Barbados Dr, Winter Park, FL 32792
800/633-6116   407/657-3776 Fax
<lithocards@aol.com>
1000 four-color cards for $390

PRIVATE ISSUE STAMPS

Custom, full-color stamps from your artwork or photos. They will not have any mailing value, but they will certainly look great on your envelope, letterhead or business card.

Anna Banana
RR 22, 3747 Highway 101, Roberts creek, BC Canada V0N 2W2
604/885-7156   604/885-7183 Fax
www.users.uniserve.ca/~sno958   <a_banana@sunshine.net>

1 stamp: 500 copies @ $150

Block of 3 stamps: 500 copies for $600 (1500 stamps @ 40¢); 1000 copies for $750

Block of 6 stamps: 500 for $850 (3000 stamps @ 28¢); 1000 copies for $1000

CARD REPS

Greeting card reps expect you to have a minimum of 18 varieties before they will rep you. They are independent contractors who represent several artists or companies, by whom they are paid a commission. They write orders for accounts in their assigned territory and send them to the manufacturer (the artist, you, in this case) to be filled.

Most large card companies sell their cards through reps. These reps often attend trade shows around the country as well as sell directly to stores.

➤ Reps take orders and get a commission from you on the orders they pass on to you. You fill the order, ship it and pay the rep.

➤ Reps generally receive 20% of their gross wholesale orders.

➤ Reps are paid 20 days after you ship to the customer for whom the rep took the order.

➤ Reps generally have exclusive sales territories. They also may have a specific industry (i.e., florist industry, children's accessory stores, etc.). A greeting card company often has two to eight reps in one area covering all the various markets.

Interview greeting card reps and check their references, just as you would a potential employee. Verify the territory they cover, length of time in business, retail accounts they call on (i.e., how many?). Is their mailing list available for you to do a promo? Do they sell other products? What trade shows do they participate in?

A small company will need 1000-2000 accounts. Marcel Schurman, as an example, has 15,000 accounts, which are handled by their own in-house reps.

An example of your income would then be: 1000 accounts x $100 sales (the minimum) = $100,000 in wholesale sales for the year. When you work on your five-year plan, you will try to anticipate future income and expenses by taking into account the number of reps you anticipate having.

Once you have a rep, be sure to remain in contact. It will mean more sales. If you have a rep who exhibits at stationery and gift shows, see if you can assist at the exhibit in some manner. Make it a win-win situation.

FINDING A CARD REP

➤ Stationery and gift shows, where reps set up booths, are good places to talk to reps.

➤ Ask your local stationery store who their reps are.

➤ Your local design center might be a place where reps have set up shop.

QUESTIONS TO ASK A POTENTIAL REP

➤ What territory does the rep cover?

➤ Number of reps in the company?

➤ How many lines do they carry? Do they mix well with yours?

➤ What is the percentage of cards vs gift lines they carry?

➤ Does the rep do any trade shows? If so, what does it cost you?

➤ Discuss types of accounts they call on (boutiques, gift stores, galleries).

➤ What is her commission?

➤ Ask for business references.

WHAT A REP NEEDS FROM AN ARTIST

➤ Sample of cards

➤ Catalogs to exhibit cards

➤ Order forms

➤ Continuous updates on any discontinued items

➤ Incentives offers

➤ New product release at least twice a year; three to four times is more common

➤ Timely shipping

➤ Timely paying of commission

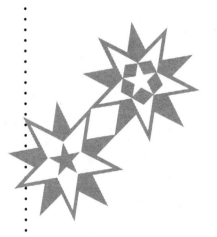

RESOURCE

The LA Gift Mart
213/749-7911
Some manufacturer's reps have showrooms there. You can study what they sell and see if your work is appropriate.

TRADE SHOWS

You will not need stock for shows. You will only show samples of the different lines for which you will be taking orders. It's best to have 24-48 designs for customers to choose from. Representing yourself at shows is a costly venture that has paid off for many artists. You could also rent a space cooperatively with a group of artists.

Try to find some niche market shows to attend, such as florist shows, dog shows, etc. One lady had an entire booth of cards at an outdoor art show. She was doing a whopping business selling her cards from $3 up.

NATIONAL TRADE SHOWS

National Stationery Show
George Little Management
800/272-SHOW
www.nationalstationeryshow.com
The main show for the US market, held in New York annually in May

Atlanta Gift & Stationery Show
404/220-3000
Second largest show of its kind in US

ORGANIZATIONS

Gift Association of America
PO Box 26696, Collegeville, PA 19426
610/831-1841
Members are generally retail store owners, wholesalers and affiliates.

Greeting Card Association
1156 15th St NW #900, Washington, DC 20005
202/393-1778
www.greetingcard.org
Directory of Greeting Card Sales Representatives *lists over 160 companies and individual sales reps in the US. $100ppd for non-members. This organization also has a variety of other useful items.*

MAILING LISTS

ArtNetwork
800/383-0677
350 greeting card reps are available for rent at $50. They come on pressure-sensitive labels for one-time usage. Call for brochure.

DIRECTORY

National Rep Group Directory
Spoor & Associates
2048 May Valley Wy, Henderson, NV 89052
800/770-7470
www.spoorconsultants.com
Lists over 2000 reps in all the major markets and has a calendar of major US gift shows and much more. $100ppd. Updated annually, in its 11th year, includes producers of trade shows, industry associations, trade publications, national reps of gifts, toys, gourmet products and decorative accessories.

CARD SUPPLIES

Clear Solutions
PO Box 2460, W Brattleboro, VT 05303
603/256-6644 603/256-8057 Fax
www.cleardisplays.com <sales@cleardisplays.com>
Manufacturer of racks for cards. Custom and regular designs.

Impact Images
4919 Windplay Dr, El Dorado Hills, CA 95702
800/233-2630 916/933-4700
www.clearbags.com
Plastic sleeves for greeting cards and original artwork. ArtNetwork uses these clear envelopes to send our biannual edition of the Encyclopedia of Living Artists. *Colored materials look great peering through.*

Rice Paper Box Co
530 Acoma St, Denver, CO 80204
877/825-8287 303/825-8287
www.ricepaperbox.com
Card boxes in a variety of styles and colors; stock and custom order

See the list of magazines in Chapter 10.

THE HANDMADE CARD

BY CONSTANCE SMITH

Many artists are starting their own greeting card businesses by making beautiful handmade greeting cards—indeed, beautiful enough to frame. Bookstores, paper stores, gift shops, museum stores, children's stores and private individuals are just the tip of the iceberg for possible markets for handmade greeting cards.

Unlike printing cards by the thousands, the low financial risk of handmade cards offers more flexibility. You will need to do lots of research before you actually hit the marketplace with your creations.

➤ You can make and sell cards from your home.

➤ Low investment. Eventually you might see that you want to go into printing cards because they are so popular.

➤ Because of their unusualness, they can be easy to sell to stores. In some cases you'll see a pin on a card as part of the design—an easily-purchased and not too expensive gift or thank-you.

ASK YOURSELF

➤ Are there other cards similar to yours on the market already? How do they sell?

➤ How are yours different enough for a store to want to carry them?

➤ Can you come in at a competitive price?

➤ What paper seems to be used most?

➤ What price ranges do you find?

➤ What sizes are the cards?

➤ What's "hot" on the market?

TIPS

➤ Verify that your card is mailable; if it has something attached like a button or pin, will it break in the mail? Your envelope may need to say in large letters, "Hand Stamp." This could be an added expense.

➤ Package fewer cards in each box to make your overall price lower, i.e., eight cards instead of 10 or 12.

➤ On the back of the card put a blurb about how it was made, tell a story, make it more interesting. Customers love reading about artists and how they create.

PRICING

Calculate the labor costs from a test run of 20 pieces. An hour is based on a 50-minute time frame. Retail needs to be 6-10 times the actual cost.

Sample budget for 1,200 greeting cards (100 dozen)

Envelopes @ .05	$ 60
Bags/boxes @ .05	$ 60
Photocopy/paper	$ 40
Cutting	$ 10
Hand-coloring	$144
Actual cost	$314

Let's take the example above. Outside costs are at $314 or $3.14 per dozen. Multiply this $3.14 x 10 to get retail price of $31.40 per dozen or $2.61 per-card retail. Not a bad price at all for a handmade card!

THE MAKE-UP OF A $2.50 CARD

Use these quantities when compiling a budget for your prospective company.

50%	Store markup	$1.25
10%	Rep commission	.25
10%	Production	.25
10%	Overhead	.25
7.5%	Promotion	.19
7.5%	Profit	.19
5%	Artwork	.12

COST TO START A BUSINESS

You will need to consider: paper, supplies such as glue and paint, envelopes, packaging (bags or boxes), inserts, labeling, printing, assembling, labor, company business cards, catalog sheets for advertising, trade journal ads, travel to trade shows. When you make your five-year business plan, be sure to include all these factors.

If you are going to print cards in four-color in small quantities, the costs will skyrocket. 1000 cards would be around 38¢ each ($375). Photocopy and then hand-paint them. You can then call them handmade cards. One artist I know hires disabled workers to help her assemble pieces that have to be repetitively created. Call your local Salvation Army for referrals.

MARKETING

Some reps sell handmade cards, but not many. You probably will have to do most of your marketing. Try to find unusual outlets for your unusual cards: coffee houses, hospital gift shops, restaurants, garden shops, record stores, florist shops, beauty salons, frame shops, health food stores, children's stores, quick-stop stores, zoos, museums, hotel shops, bookstores, New Age shops, tourist shops, etc. Find your niche market and go for it!

RECOMMENDED READING

Books and Cards by Jean Kropper
Davis Publication Books for Art Education
50 Portland St, Worcester, MA 01608-2013
800/533-2837   508/754-7201
A thorough examination of the basic techniques, tools and materials, setting the stage for creative exploration and experimentation. $24.95

The Complete Guide to Greeting Card Design & Illustration By Eva Szels
North Light Books
800/289-0963
This book features published samples, tips and insider information on creating successful card designs.

Designing for Greeting Cards
P F Design
2101 Valley View Dr, Rocky River, OH 44116
This essential handbook contains advice on layout, research, selling, copyright and much more. $14.95 + $3 shipping.

❑ Investigate what greeting cards are being sold at several local stores.

❑ Attend a trade show to study the market.

❑ Think about your target niche market: is your card made from 100% recycled materials? Hemp? Vintage buttons, beads or fabric?

❑ Research mailing requirements for your cards, then label your envelopes accordingly.

❑ Will your cards contain text? Do you need to find a writer?

ACTION PLAN

Use the answers to the questions at left to create your action plan.

1. _____

2. _____

3. _____

4. _____

5. _____

6. _____

7. _____

8. _____

9. _____

10. _____

Chapter 9
Home-Grown Calendars

Planning

Design

Printing

Marketing and distribution

We all name ourselves. We call ourselves artists. Nobody asks us. Nobody says you are or you aren't.

   Ad Reinhardt

PLANNING

It's highly suggested you search to find a calendar publisher to produce your calendar. To give you an idea of what it takes and to understand what an established calendar publisher risks, we will proceed in the following pages through the calendar publishing process.

Marketing a calendar is one of the most difficult tasks you could assign yourself. Planning a calendar is a long project. A store has only three main months to sell to individuals. Calendar sales are dead after March 1.

As you know from your own household and office, you probably have a multitude of calendars. Many people give calendars for Christmas presents; theoretically, one-third of calendars purchased are given as gifts, wall calendars being the most popular style.

REASONS TO SELF-PUBLISH A CALENDAR

➤ You have a huge client base from selling your art for years. You have the addresses in your database.

➤ You are working with an art organization or company who is guaranteeing sales of a certain quantity.

➤You have a particular group of retailers (tennis pro shops, equine shops) to whom to wholesale.

Though you might be printing a much smaller quantity than the established publishers, your retail price needs to be in line with theirs. Without a distributor, it means a lot of knocking on doors.

Calendar runs smaller than 20K are considered small.

➤ Who is your target market?

➤ Can you find a distributor?

➤ Do you know what packaging (and the cost) you will need?

➤ Is your design a similar size to most standard calendars so it will display on store shelves easily?

Look at competitors' calendars: What works? What don't you like? Where are they distributed: bookstores, newsstands, gift shops, department stores, catalogs? Go to a neighboring city to see what they have displayed and how it might be different.

WHAT COMPRISES A GOOD CALENDAR?

It's a must for a self-published calendar to be "different." The large calendar publishers and distributors have the market for commonplace distribution—yours must be exotic in some manner. Check out today's calendar themes in bookstores, specialty shops, museum stores and boutiques. Think of a theme that you can build on year after year. Once you develop a calendar, you want to continue.

➤ Depending on what your calendar's theme is, you will want to list some of the special events related to it on the daily square spaces. Do a bit of research. Make your calendar thorough and unusual. Be forewarned: too many listings in the square make for a hectic-looking calendar.

➤ Many calendars incorporate moon phases into their boxes. You'll need to do a bit of research if you want this on your calendar.

➤ What is the most common size?

➤ Which sizes, styles get best position on sales racks?

➤ What are the most common types of paper used? How does that affect sales?

➤ Are there a lot of other calendars with the same theme as you are planning?

➤ Make a list of prices of various calendars.

MOCK-UP CALENDAR

➤ To select the final 12 images (the cover is repeated inside), you will need to start with about 20-25 possibilities.

➤ Make a mock-up of your final choices. Review it for awhile. Don't make any rash decisions. Pass it around to friends as well as local business professionals—people who will eventually buy. Listen to their comments. Get their opinion. Study their reaction. It's a good introduction to taking their order later.

DESIGN

SPECIAL INGREDIENTS

You might have noticed that most every item you buy has a barcode on it these days. Calendars require a different style of barcode than groceries or toys. Books take even another kind of barcode. These codes make it easy for an item to be scanned in a retail outlet. In the case of books and calendars, these bar codes are created from the numbers assigned to publishers.

ISSN

You will use an ISSN number for serials or periodicals, such as calendars and magazines. ArtNetwork's ISSN number for *ArtSource Quarterly* is 1064-6620. If we sold this publication in stores (we sell it only by subscription), we would convert this number into a barcode (sometimes called a UPC barcode) and place it on our back cover, so it would be easy for a scanner to tabulate the price and inventory.

RESOURCE

ISSN
202/707-6333 Fax
<issn@loc.gov>

ISBN

You will use an ISBN for books. ArtNetwork's ISBN number for books always begins with 0-940899-. The last three numbers are the only numbers that change for each book. In the case of this book, the last three numbers are 77-2. Look on the back cover of this book and you will see how this ISBN number has been changed into a barcode so your local bookstore can easily keep inventory on this book.

RESOURCE

RR Bowker
Don Riseborough
121 Chanlong Rd, New Providence, NJ 07494
908/464-6800
www.isbn.org <isbn-san@bowker.com>

PRODUCTION SCHEDULE

Artwork needs to be ready 18 months in advance.

Fall (year previous to sales): Mock-up starts.

Winter (year previous to sales): Camera-ready material 11 months in advance

December (year previous to sales): Mock-up is finalized.

Spring: Mock-ups are shown at shows. Orders are taken.

Summer: Printing is finished. Orders are sent

October/November/December: Calendars are in the stores for three months.

Depending on your final quantity, overseas printing can save you lots of money. Sometimes a job is half the cost that it would be if printed in the US. In this day and age with e-mail and overnight deliveries, it is as simple to work with a printer in the Orient as it is working with a printer on the "mainland." The only step that takes longer is the shipping. Because it's by boat it can take four to six weeks. Add on time for clearing customs (one week) and for shipping to your offices (another week). If your quantity is going to be smaller than 2500, then print in the U.S.

PRINTING PREP

➤ You can use 35mm slides for reproduction if piece is not larger than 8x10". Use a 4x5 tranny if reproduction will be larger than 8x10".

➤ Check the transparency carefully for color match and clarity.

➤ Separations can be a large part of the final printing cost, ranging from $45 - 125 for each piece.

PRINTING BUDGET

Total cost for 1000 could be about $5 each. Triple this individual cost for retail price: $14.95, an average cost for a well-made calendar. You will wholesale for only $7.48 (a $2.48 profit on each calendar) or $2000 for the year. Thus, you need to think in terms of longevity and selling more and more each year.

PRINTING

See page 197 for printers and print brokers.

Consider also that in future years, your costs will go down because your quantities will rise; thus your profit margin will be larger. Your original work prices will often rise at that point too. Maybe you should publish a limited-edition calendar and charge a bit more! Be creative.

Each year, as long as you keep working on it, you should sell more calendars. Think of it as promotion and a building process. If you combine it with promotion of a new limited-edition or open-edition print each year, all your customers will be happy.

TIPS

➤ Remember that the reproduction on your calendar is an inexpensive type of reproduction—it is not a giclée or limited-edition print costing $500. Be fussy about the color but don't be ridiculous. Save your energy for promoting your calendar.

➤ For the first printing, just do a small print run—500.

➤ Keep your printing costs down with a common size of calendar (9x12″). This size gives the user plenty of space to write notes on, an important feature of any calendar. If you keep the size and layout the same year after year it is much easier to lay out annually.

➤ Sell at arts and crafts shows, local bookshops, gift shops and boutiques. Perhaps this can be your foot in the door for originals as well as prints.

➤ Eventually contact reps for distribution. If you have prints or cards to go along with your calendar, it always makes it more welcome to them.

➤ When creating your art, consider using a 9x12″ size, twice the size of a card, or even 18x24″, which reduces and fits perfectly.

What will you do with returns? Maybe you can send to corporate art consultants, etc., for promotional tools.

CALENDAR PRINTERS

American Custom Calendars
6221 E Park Ave, Libertyville, IL 60048
800/828-8225

Banta Media Services
675 Brighton Beach Rd, Menasha, WI 54952
414/751-7639

Donihe Graphics
766 Brookside Dr, Kingsport, TN 37660
800/251-0337

Teldon Calendars
250 H St, PMB 8000, Blaine, WA 98230-4033
800/755-9970

PRINTER BROKERS FOR THE ORIENT

Imago
Gregory Lee
31952 Camino Capistranto #C22, San Juan Capistrano, CA 92675
949/661-5998
<glee@imagousa.com>

InterPress
Laura Jaffe
2854 Coastal Hwy, St Augustine FL 32084
888/338-7726   877/747-1775 Fax
<interpress@earthlink.net>
Rep for a Hong Kong printer. We have printed with them twice and intend to print with them again (for our four-color jobs). They are excellent printers and very easy to work with—made our life easy!

As a self publisher, more than likely you will need to become a self-distributor. Unless you have an outlandishly original and super-hot idea for your calendar, your efforts to promote your singular calendar will probably prove difficult.

MARKETING AND DISTRIBUTION

DIRECT MAIL

If you have a very specific targeted market (tennis players, golfers, abstract art enthusiasts, etc.), you will possibly be successful through direct mail. With such a low-cost item and high-cost promotion, your percentage of purchasers has to be high. If you have previous customers who have purchased your originals, or signed your guest book at an outdoor show, then those are good potential buyers. Without having previous contact with this direct-mail list, your percentages of follow-through purchases will probably go down. You might not even be able to cover your costs.

This is why, if you are going to start marketing a calendar, you must plan to do this for consecutive years—even if the first year is not as successful as you had hoped. Each year you will find more customers, more interest, and you will get more PR. If your calendar is trendy enough, you might even be able to get on a radio or TV talk show. It really helps at that point if it is selling in the mainstream stores (which means having a mainstream distributor) where people will most easily find it.

• You will also need to be able to accept VISA/Master Card/Am/Ex.

• You will need someone to answer a phone—probably an 800 number.

• You will need proper packaging for shipping.

DIRECT MAIL TIPS

➤ Keep the weight of your mailer under an ounce.

➤ Have the final size fit the USPS standard mailing size, no longer than 11.5 ", no higher than 6". A design that is unique might cost you more to mail. Always check with the post office before you print. For instance, if you design a 6x6" card, it will cost 45¢ to mail; a 10x6" costs only 34¢.

➤ Use a self-mailer—there will be no envelope costs and no sealing time. If you design a beuaitful mailer, everyone will see it.

➤ Offer a money-back guarantee. It makes purchasers feel more secure.

RETURN POLICIES

It's better for small publishers (yourself!) to work with specialty stores rather than bookstores, due to bookstores' return policies. Many stores have large quantities of returns. With a dated item such as a calendar, this is no good!

Try to get a non-returnable agreement if you sell to stores directly by giving them a slightly bigger discount. Expect to sell 10-20 in any given store.

You could donate these returned calendars to organizations: school, charity, nursing home, hospital, scout troop. Indeed, this might lead to sales in the future and shows you're a "good citizen."

TRADE SHOWS

American Booksellers Association Convention

828 S Broadway, Tarrytown, NY 10591

914/591-2665

The American Booksellers Association show—Book Expo America—is held each year in June. There are two new venues to market calendars at this show: "Calendar MarketPlace" and "Calendar Expo International." You do not have to attend the show to exhibit your calendars. Call for exhibition prices and deadlines. This organization also gives National Calendar Awards each year sponsored by the Calendar Marketing Association, the industry's premier competition. In the February/March issue of their magazine, they list distributors' calendar catalogs.

National Stationery Show

George Little Management

800/222-SHOW

Held annually in mid-May in New York City

WHOLESALING

If you wholesale 50% and retail 50% of your calendars, you will make more money. By wholesaling you will sell much more quantity, ultimately lowering your cost per calendar.

Start with local galleries, then spread to other venues and areas.

DISTRIBUTORS

Ingram

615/793-5000

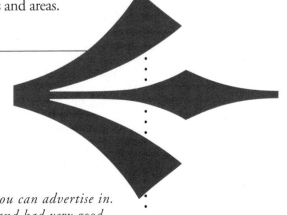

Baker & Taylor

PO Box 734, Somerville, NJ 08876-0734

908/541-7493

www.baker-taylor.com

Get information on their many publications that you can advertise in. ArtNetwork has advertised books in some of them and had very good results.

Publishers Weekly
245 W 17th St, New York, NY 10011
212/463-6758   212/463-6631
This magazine will keep you abreast of new books, calendars and cover designs. March is the calendar issue. $6.50 per issue.

REPS

Sunbelt Publications
Diana Lindsay
1250 Fayette St, El Cajon, CA 92020
619/258-4911   619/258-4916 Fax
Wholesaler whose customers include national chain stores and various specialty outlets. Send your calendar mock-up in plenty of time for them to consider it.

ORGANIZATION

Calendar Market Association
Dick Mikes
710 E Ogden Ave #600, Naperville, IL 60563
630/579-264   630/369-2488 Fax
www.calendarmarketplace.com <cma@b-online.com>
Call or write for information on what this association offers. Carry a book entitled How to Publish/Market Your Calendar. *$69.95 + shipping.*

BOOK

Calendar Design + Graphics
This collection of art layouts will help you discover all the artistry, creativity and imaginative use of technology and art put into calendars today. Out-of-print, so look for it at your library.

WEB SITE

www.2003calendarlayouts.com
You can download 13 editable high-resolution layouts for $19.95.

❑ Calculate the costs of printing a calendar.

Retail buyers:

_____

_____

_____

Wholesale buyers:

_____

_____

_____

PR possibilities:

_____

_____

_____

Advertising venues:

_____

_____

_____

Brainstorm calendar themes _____

_____

_____

_____

Who are your niche markets for your selected themes? ____

_____

_____

_____

ACTION PLAN

Use the answers to the questions at left to create your action plan.

1. _____

2. _____

3. _____

4. _____

5. _____

6. _____

7. _____

8. _____

9. _____

10. _____

Chapter 10
Contacts

Licensing agents

Art publishers

Book publishers

Resources

Sample contract

Art is really a battle.
Edgar Degas

Agent Andy

Andrew Abrams
221 Orient Wy, Lyndhurst, NJ 07071
201/933-8098
www.agentandy.com <info@agentandy.com>

Role in licensing industry: licensing agent; career coach, royalty sharing or for hire
We handle contracts with living artists.
Particular market you target: giftware and decorative accessories
How often do you review work: weekly
We do not have a review committee.
Specific styles of work you prefer: all
We are: actively seeking new artists, seeking established artists through referral, reviewing unsolicited slides from fine artists, filing slides for possible future publication
Artists can contact us by: submitting portfolio for review by mail (with SASE if you want it returned), e-mailing portfolio
Number of artists we work with presently: 300
Tips for those contacting us: check web site first
Best time of year to submit portfolio: year-round
We prefer to review: 8.5x11″ or smaller
Trade shows we attend: Surtex, ArtExpo, Licensing/NY, gift shows

AJM Marketing Enterprises

Anthony Marsiglia
1515 Woodfield Rd, Schaumburg IL 60173-6046
<ajmlicense@aol.com>

Air Waves Inc

Heather McGarry
7787 Graphics Wy, Lewis Center, OH 43035
740/548-1200 740/548-1212 Fax
www.airwavesinc.com <hncgarry@airwavesinc.com>

Role in licensing industry: largest licensee for applied graphics
We handle contracts with living artists.
Particular market you target: all
How often do you review work: monthly
We have a review committee.
Specific styles of work you prefer: various, suitable art for apparel

We are: actively seeking new artists, seeking established artists through referral, reviewing unsolicited slides from fine artists, filing slides for possible future publication
Artists can contact us by: submitting portfolio for review by mail, e-mailing portfolio
Number of artists we work with presently: 60-70
Tips for those contacting us: ask for our art submittal form
Best time of year to submit portfolio: Spring/Fall
We prefer to review: color copies
Trade shows we attend: Surtex, ArtExpo
Trade shows we exhibit at: Licensing/NY

Alaska Momma Inc

Shirley Henschel
303 Fifth Ave #2009, New York NY 10016-6652
<licensing@alaskamomma.com>

AmI! Art Makers International

Kay Yearick
PO Box 67185, St Pete Beach, FL 33736-7185
727/360-9700 727/360-9699 Fax
www.artmakersintl.com <amiart@ij.net>

Andrews McMeel Universal

Denise Clark
4520 Main St, Kansas City, MO 64111-7701
816/932-6680 816/932-6689 Fax
www.uexpress.com <dclark@amuniversal.com>

Ansco Photo

Frank Gruzewski
1801 Touhy, Elk Grove Village, IL 60007
847/981-0108

Aprilminded

Maryann Roberts-Green
677 Palmer Ave, Holmdel, NJ 07733
732/787-8959 732/495-7868 Fax
www.aprilminded.com

Art Merchandising & Media
Kristin Ehring
Munchnerstrasse 20, Unterfohring 85774 Germany
www.artmm-ag.com <info@artmm-ag.com>

Art in Motion
Carrie Farina
2000 Hartley Ave, Coquitlam BC V3K 6W5 Canada
604/525-3900 604/525-6166 Fax
www.artinmotion.com <cfarina@artinmotion.com>

ArtBrands Consumer Products
Elisa Valentino
25 Nassau Blvd, Garden City, NY 11530
516/742-0040 516/741-4761 Fax
<artbrands@aol.com>

Artistic License
Shary Klamer
10537 Clearwood Ct, LA, CA 90077
310/475-6202 310/470-2972 Fax
www.artisticlicensing.com <artisticlic2@aol.com>

Arts Uniq'
Carol White
PO Box 3085, Cookeville, TN 38502-3085
800/223-5020
<licensing@aulicensing.com>

B Creative Inc
Scott Gardiner
536 Pantops Ctr #317, Charlottesville, VA 22911-8665
www.bcreative.com <sgardiner@bcreative.com>

Role in licensing industry: agent/licensor
We handle contracts with living artists.
Particular market you target: many styles
How often do you review work: daily
We do not have a review committee.
Specific styles of work you prefer: all
We are: actively seeking new artists, seeking established artists through referral, reviewing unsolicited slides from fine artists

Artists can contact us by: join as a creative member on www.bcreative.com
Number of artists we work with presently: hundreds
Tips for those contacting us: go on-line to our site
Best time of year to submit portfolio: year-round
We prefer to review: on-line
Trade shows we attend: ArtExpo, Licensing/NY
Trade shows we exhibit at: Licensing/NY

Bell Consulting
James Bell
25 Van Zant St #9B, Norwalk, CT 06855
203/854-9693 203/854-9848 Fax
<jimbell@belllicensing.com>

Bookstop Literacy Agency
Kendra Marcus
67 Meadow View Rd, Orinda, CA 94563-3246
925/254-2664
www.bookstopliteracy.com

Role in licensing industry: agent
We handle contracts with living artists.
Particular market you target: children's book illustration
How often do you review work: daily
We have a review committee.
We are: actively seeking new artists, reviewing unsolicited slides from fine artists
Artists can contact us by: submitting portfolio for review by mail
Number of artists we work with presently: 20
Tips for those contacting us: send copies of your range of styles; show ability to portray characters
We prefer to review: color copies
Trade shows we attend: Surtex, Licensing/NY

Bouncynet Inc
200 E Broward Blvd #1920, Ft Lauderdale, FL 33301

Brand Ventures Group

Joshua Brand
PO Box 486, 15 Girard St, Marlboro, NJ 07464
732/617-1234 732/536-9047 Fax
www.brandven.com <jmbrand@aol.com>

Role in licensing industry: agent
We handle contracts with living artists.
Particular market you target: many
We are: actively seeking new artists, seeking established artists through referral
Artists can contact us by: submitting portfolio for review by mail
Number of artists we work with presently: 12
Best time of year to submit portfolio: July - September
We prefer to review: prints or slides
Trade shows we attend: Surtex, ArtExpo, Licensing/NY, various other shows

Brown & Bigelow Licensing Co

Teresa Roussin
345 Plato Blvd, St Paul, MN 55107-1269
<troussin@brownandbigelow.com>

the buffalo works

Joanne Olds
PO Box 621, Wayzata, MN 55391
952/475-3013   952/475-3016 Fax
www.thebuffaloworks.com
<jolds@thebuffaloworks.com>

Bugbee & Assoc

Robin Bugbee
94 Blackstone Blvd, Providence, RI 02906

C S Engel & Assoc

Carol Engel
211 E 77th St, New York, NY 10021
212/737-0544 212/772-1284 Fax
<cengel@nyc.rr.com>

Candle on the Web

Robert Martin
PO Box 6039, Kingston, NY 12401

Carte Blanche Licensing

Andy Jakobschuk
15 Kodiak Crest, Toronto, Ont M3J 3E5 Canada

Consumer Licensing Corp

Dan Gabbay
325 Kennedy Dr #1331, Hauppauge, NY 11788

Contact Representation

Elizabeth Smith
243 Stanford Dr, San Antonio, TX 78212

Cop Corp

Rob Posta
1365 York Ave #38K, New York, NY 10021
212/327-4190 212/879-2108 Fax
<posts524@aol.com>

Role in licensing industry: retail consultants/agent/international licensing
We handle contracts with living artists.
Particular market you target: all markets
How often do you review work: daily
We have a review committee.
We are: actively seeking new artists, seeking established artists through referral
Artists can contact us by: submitting portfolio for review by mail, e-mailing portfolio
Number of artists we work with presently: 25
Tips for those contacting us: understand what art licensing is
Best time of year to submit portfolio: anytime
We prefer to review: slides/photos
Trade shows we attend: Surtex, ArtExpo, Licensing/NY, most shows
Trade shows we exhibit at: Licensing/NY

Creatif Licensing Corp

Mary Silverman
31 Old Town Crossing, Mt Kisco, NY 10549-4030
914/241-6211 914/666-4794 Fax
www.creatifusa.com <art@creatifusa.com>

Role in licensing industry: licensing agents for artists
We handle contracts with living artists.
How often do you review work: monthly
We do not have a review committee.
We are: seeking established artists through referral
Artists can contact us by: submitting portfolio for review by mail, e-mailing portfolio
Number of artists we work with presently: 15
Tips for those contacting us: include a SASE
Best time of year to submit portfolio: year-round
We prefer to review: color copies
Trade shows we attend: Surtex, ArtExpo, Licensing/NY
Trade shows we exhibit at: Licensing/NY

Creative Connection

Laurie High
PO Box 253, Gibson Island, MD 21056
410/360-5981 410/255-8889 Fax
www.cciart.com <mail@cciart.com>

D Parks & Associates

Ayako Parks
28512 Avenida Placida, San Juan Capistrano, CA 92675
www.art-licensing.com <info@art-licensing.com>

Dan-Dee International Ltd

Gary Holcomb
106 Harbor Dr, Jersey City, NJ 07305

e-Global Bridge Inc

Danny Han
169-17 Northern Blvd, Flushing, NY 11358

E S Originals

Pam Glazer
450 W 33rd St #9Fl, New York, NY 10001

Engravable U

Jon Lanenga
945 Pennsylvania, Winter Park, FL 32789

Frends & Assoc

Jane Frendberg
10274 Braemar Dr, Powell, OH 43065
614/766-9934 614/760-9951 Fax
www.frendslicensing.com <jfrendberg@columbus.rr.com>

Role in licensing industry: consultant, agent
We handle contracts with living artists.
Particular market you target: all home decor and paper, party, publications
Specific styles of work you prefer: all
We are: reviewing unsolicited slides from fine artists
Artists can contact us by: submitting portfolio for review by mail, e-mailing portfolio
Number of artists we work with presently: 2
Best time of year to submit portfolio: any time
We prefer to review: color copies, photos, transparencies, slides
Trade shows we attend: Surtex, Licensing/NY
Trade shows we exhibit at: Licensing/NY

Ginsey Industries

Harry Haber
281 Benigno Blvd, Bellmawr, NJ 08031

Hadley Licensing

Mary Marshall
11300 Hampshire Ave S, Bloomington, MN 55438
800/927-0660
<macsm@hadley.com>

Hallmark Licensing
Janet Broll
2440 Pershing Rd #300, Kansas City, MO 64141-6266

Hasbro Inc
Leslie Sanders
1027 Newport Ave, Pawtucket, RI 02861-2500
<lsanders@hasbro.com>

I Licensing
Kara O'Dell
1145 Sunrise Greetings Ct, Bloomington, IN 47402
812/336-9900   812/336-8712 Fax
www.interart.com   <kodell@interart.com>

In Gear Corp
Larry Gutkin
13518 Abbott Ct, Buffalo Grove, IL 60089

Indigo Gate
Gifford B Browne II
1 Pegasus Dr, Colts Neck, NJ 07722-1490
732/577-9333   732/577-9393 Fax
<indigogate@aol.com>
Representing Anthony P Mauro (children's writer), Daryl Lynn O'Connell (inspirational writer), Ms Michal Sparks (artist, illustrator, designer, author), Ms Lisa Hollister Sorensen (photographer) and more. "When a property proves itself over time, it has the potential to become a brand; one that people will associate with specific values and experience."

Intercontinental Greetings
George Medina
176 Madison Ave, New York, NY 10016-5100
212/683-5830   212/779-8564 Fax
www.intercontinental-ltd.com
<lnterny@intercontinental-ltd.com>

Internatural Designs
Sarah Esser
5100 Highway 169 N, Minneapolis, MN 55428

Julie & Co
Julie Wood
12204 Buena Vista, Leawood, KS 66209
913/451-5775   913/451-8162 Fax
<jwood@qni.com>

Lally Inc
Kathy Lally
7033 Wooddale Ave S, Minneapolis, MN 55435
952/926-2374   952/926-2303 Fax
www.lallyinc.com

Kathy Lally brings more than 19 years experience in her business. She is president of Twin Cities Licensing Club. Lally Inc continuously reviews artist submissions. Submit 10-12 color copies/ photographs/CD/slides/transparencies that represent your style of work. Make sure each has your name and address clearly indicated. Also a short bio or descriptive letter and materials. Indicate any previous licensing experience or representation. Send materials with SASE. All materials will be reviewed. You will receive a response by phone or mail.

L & G Licensing
Liz Stahler
1400 Chautauqua Blvd, Pacific Palisades, CA 90272
310/454-8825   209/844-9718 Fax
<lng@earthlink.net>

LDM Enterprises
Lisa McGuckin
7137 Tern Pl, Carlsbad, CA 92009
760/918-9813   760/918-9814 Fax
<ldment2001@aol.com>

Artist liaison: Chris Bubany
Role in licensing industry: licensing agent

We review work from: illustrators
We handle contracts with living artists.
Particular market you target: housewares, paper products
We are: actively seeking new artists
Artists can contact us by: submitting e-mail portfolio
Number of artists we work with presently: 1
Tips for those contacting us: telephone or e-mail
Trade shows we attend: Surtex, Licensing/NY
Trade shows we exhibit at: Licensing/NY, other
California- and Arizona-based

LKT Creative
Louise Ternay
119 Birch Ave, Bala Cynwyd, PA 19004-3010
610/667-8626   610/664-1379 Fax
<lternay@aol.com>

Role in licensing industry: art agent
We handle contracts with living artists.
Specific styles of work you prefer: all types
We are: actively seeking new artists, seeking established
artists through referral, reviewing unsolicited slides from
fine artists, filing slides for possible future publication
Artists can contact us by: submitting portfolio for review
by mail, e-mailing portfolio
Number of artists we work with presently: 800
Best time of year to submit portfolio: any time
We prefer to review: non-returnable good color, clear, flat
art
Trade shows we attend: Surtex, ArtExpo, Licensing/NY,
Stationery Show, NY gift show
Trade shows we exhibit at: Licensing/NY

Laurie Lambert & Associates
Laurie Stokes
9600 Stone Masters Dr, Loveland, OH 45140
513/774-9777   513/774-8603 Fax
www.lambertassociatesinc.com   <lalasc@aolc.om>

Legend Licensing
Leonard Traub
301 W Hallandale Beach Blvd, Hallandale, FL 33009
954/454-0133
www.legendlicensing.com

Licensing Brands International
Christine Annechino
23 E 22 St #5Fl, New York, NY 10010
212/614-7067   212/583-1448
<licensingbrands@att.net>

Licensing Group
Danny Simon
8455 Beverly Blvd #508, Los Angeles, CA 90048
323/653-2700   323/653-2771 Fax
www.thelicensinggroup.com   <tlgla@aol.com>

Licensing Management
Mark Stevens
6965 El Camino Real #105-191, Carlsbad, CA 92009
760/633-3891

Licensing Management
Andrew Maconie
Goods Corner, Mill Lane Burley, Ringwood, Hants BH24
4HP England
www.lmiuk.com   <lmiuk@aol.com>

Lifestyle Licensing International
Dean Berko
Box 25487, Honolulu, HI 96825
808/394-0438   808/394-0462 Fax
www.lifestylelicensing.com   <lifestyledean@aol.com>

Role in licensing industry: agency
We handle contracts with living artists.
Specific styles of work you prefer: various
We are: actively seeking new artists, seeking established
artists through referral, reviewing unsolicited slides from
fine artists
Artists can contact us by: calling to arrange a personal
interview to show portfolio, submitting portfolio for
review by mail, e-mailing portfolio
Number of artists we work with presently: 8
Best time of year to submit portfolio: any time
We prefer to review: web sites
Trade shows we attend: Surtex, ArtExpo, Licensing/NY
Trade shows we exhibit at: Licensing/NY

Linda McDonald Inc
Linda McDonald
5200 Park Rd #104, Charlotte, NC 28209
704/370-0057   704/370-0058 Fax
www.lindamcdonald.com   <lindamcdonaldinc@msn.com>

Looking Good Licensing
Tim Good
15 N Sawyer Hill Rd, New Preston, CT 06777
860/868-1075   860/868-1077 Fax
www.lookinggoodlicensing.com
<tim@lookinggoodlicensing.com>

M4 Media Beratungs-und
Matthais Gottschalk
Frankfurter Ring 105, 80807 Munich Germany
<mfourmedia@aol.com>

McAllister Inc
Liane McAllister
181 E 73 St, New York, NY 10021
212/835-0716

MHS Licensing
Marty Degelbaum
10590 Wayzata Blvd #260, Minneapolis, MN 55305
952/544-1377   952/544-8663 Fax
www.mhslicensing.com   <nicole@mhslicensing.com>

Role in licensing industry: art licensing agency
We handle contracts with living artists.
Particular market you target: all
Specific styles of work you prefer: every style
We are: actively seeking new artists, reviewing unsolicited slides from fine artists, filing slides for possible future projects
Artists can contact us by: submitting portfolio for review by mail, e-mailing portfolio
Number of artists we work with presently: 14
Tips for those contacting us: review our web site for submission guidelines
Best time of year to submit portfolio: year-round

We prefer to review: color copies
Trade shows we attend: Surtex, Licensing/NY: we attend 20 shows annually
Trade shows we exhibit at: Surtex, Licensing/NY

Mill Pond Licensing
Angela
310 Center Ct, Venice, FL 34292
941/497-6020   941/492-6983 Fax
www.millpond.com   <millpondlicensing@yahoo.com>

Role in licensing industry: agent/publisher
We handle contracts with living artists.
Particular market you target: fine art
How often do you review work: monthly
We have a review committee.
Specific styles of work you prefer: realistic
We are: actively seeking new artists, seeking established artists through referral, filing slides for possible future publication
Artists can contact us by: submitting portfolio for review by mail
Number of artists we work with presently: 45
Tips for those contacting us: send SASE for return of materials
Best time of year to submit portfolio: any time
We prefer to review: slides
Trade shows we attend: Surtex, ArtExpo, Licensing/NY
Trade shows we exhibit at: Licensing/NY

Mosaic Licensing
Valerie Adams
2500 Bisso Ln #500, Concord, CA 94520
925/689-9930   925/356-0433 Fax
www.mosaiclicensing.com   <val@mosaiclicensing.com>

Role in licensing industry: licensing agent
We handle contracts with living artists.
Particular market you target: all
Specific styles of work you prefer: artwork that lends itself to decorative home products, i.e., dinnerware, textiles, posters
We are: seeking established artists through referral, reviewing unsolicited slides from fine artists
Artists can contact us by: submitting portfolio for review by mail

Number of artists we work with presently: 6
Tips for those contacting us: 10-15 color copies or printed material and artist information. Keep letter short and to the point.
Best time of year to submit portfolio: anytime
Trade shows we attend: Surtex, Licensing/NY, all home, gift and stationery trade shows nationally
Trade shows we exhibit at: Surtex, Licensing/NY

PM Design Group Inc
Monica Dietrich
PO box 1485, Bethlehem, PA 18016-1485
610/867-1771   610/867-6578 Fax
www.pmdesigngroup.com   <pmdietrich@aol.com>

Role in licensing industry: licensing agent
We handle contracts with living artists.
Particular market you target: decorative
How often do you review work: once a month
We have a review committee.
Specific styles of work you prefer: traditional
We are: seeking established artists through referral
Artists can contact us by: e-mailing portfolio
Number of artists we work with presently: 12+
Tips for those contacting us: check our web site to see if there's a fit
Best time of year to submit portfolio: doesn't matter
Trade shows we attend: Surtex, ArtExpo, Licensing/NY
Trade shows we exhibit at: Surtex, Licensing/NY

Porterfield's
Lance Klass
5 Mountain Rd, Concord, NH 03301
603/228-1864   603/228-1888 Fax
www.porterfieldsfineart.com   <porterfields@mediaone.net>

Role in licensing industry: fine art licensing agent
We handle contracts with living artists.
How often do you review work: daily
We have a review committee.
Specific styles of work you prefer: varies
We are: actively seeking new artists, seeking established artists through referral, reviewing unsolicited slides from fine artists
Artists can contact us by: submitting portfolio for review by mail with SASE, e-mailing portfolio

Number of artists we work with presently: 35
Tips for those contacting us: send SASE
Best time of year to submit portfolio: year-round
We prefer to review: color copies

PromoVision
Jane Putch
11361 Ovada Pl #4, Los Angeles, CA 90049
310/440-0720
www.promo-vision.com

Ready Worldwide
Don Lancaster
2562 Ambling Cir, Crofton, MD 21114
410/271-0888

Rights International Group
Robert Hazaga
463 First St #3C, Hoboken, NJ 07030-1859
201/239-8118   201/222-0694 Fax
www.rightsinternational.com
<rhazaga@rightsinternational.com>

Role in licensing industry: agent
We handle contracts with living artists.
Particular market you target: prints, posters, cards, calendars, textiles
How often do you review work: all the time
Specific styles of work you prefer: see our web site
We are: actively seeking new artists, seeking established artists through referral, reviewing unsolicited slides from fine artists, filing slides for possible future publication
Artists can contact us by: submitting portfolio for review by mail, e-mailing portfolio
Number of artists we work with presently: 25
Best time of year to submit portfolio: year-round
Trade shows we attend: Surtex, ArtExpo, Licensing/NY

Rosenthal Presents
Elise Rosenthal
3850 Eddington Ave, Calabasas, CA 91302
818/222-5445   818/222-5650 Fax

Schurman Fine Papers
Karen Goodlow
500 Chadbourne, Fairfield, CA 94533
707/428-0200   707/428-0641
www.schurman.com   <kareng@schurman.com>

Sharpe Co
Charles Day
101 Red Cedar Dr #2, Incline Village, NV 89451
775/833-1335   775/833-1336 Fax

Somerset House
Daniel Klepper
PO Box 444, Marathon, TX 79842
800/235-0021   915/386-4155 Fax
www.somersetlicensing.com
<dklepper@somersethouse.com>

Strategic Alliance Associates
Robert Sanfilippo
707 Skokie Blvd #600, Northbrook, IL 60062
847/509-2744   847/509-2743 Fax
www.saa-licensing.com   <rsanf@saa-licensing.com>

Suzanne Cruise Creative Services
Suzanne Cruise
7199 W 98th Ter #110, Overland Park, KS 66212
913/648-2190   913/648-2110 Fax
www.cruisecreative.com   <artagent@cruisecreative.com>

Synchronicity
Cynthia Hall Domine
402 Lafayette Center, Kennebunk, ME 04043
207/985-4400   207/985-4488 Fax
www.synclicensing.com   <cynthia@synclicensing.com>

Role in licensing industry: retail consultants/agent
We handle contracts with living artists.
Particular market you target: all
How often do you review work: daily

Specific styles of work you prefer: marketable!!
We are: actively seeking new artists, seeking established artists through referral, reviewing unsolicited slides from fine artists
Artists can contact us by: submitting portfolio for review by mail, e-mailing portfolio
Number of artists we work with presently: 10
Tips for those contacting us: e-mail or regular mail
Best time of year to submit portfolio: anytime
We prefer to review: print or via the web
Trade shows we attend: Surtex, Licensing/NY, stationery, home furnishing
Trade shows we exhibit at: Licensing/NY

THQ Inc
Germaine Gioia
27001 Agoura Rd #325, Calabasas Hills, CA 91301
818/223-3229
www.thq.com   <jlapin@thq.com>

Take One
Jim Sauter
12629 N Tatum Blvd #207, Phoenix, AZ 85032
602/997-4069   602/997-2888 Fax
<slaes@cineart.com>

Tangle Inc
Richard Zawitz
365 Moncada Wy, San Francisco, CA 94127
415/777-3808   415/586-4133 Fax
www.tangletoys.com   <info@tangleinc.com>

The Copyrights Group
Karen Addison
Manor Barn Milton NR Banbury, Oxford OX15 4HH
England
440/1295-721188

The Licensing Co North America

Andrea Cardillo
420 Lexington Ave #855, New York, NY 10170
646/485-4330
<andrea@us.thelicensingcompany.com>

Trade Marketing Services

Peggy Vicioso
22431-B-160 Antonio Pkwy #256, Rancho Santa Margarita, CA 92688
949/766-7855 949/766-7854 Fax
www.trademarketingservices.com
<pvicioso@trademarketingservices.com>

TransWorld Concepts

Richard Glassman
13E East St, Bound Brook, NJ 08805
732/537-6006 732/537-6005 Fax
www.transworldconcepts.com
<rglassman@transworldconcepts.com>

Why Not Licensing

Cate Smith
1593 Torbett Rd, Spring City, Tn 37381
423/365-6810
www.trywhynot.com <cat@trywhynot.com>

Role in licensing industry: consultant, agent, product analyst
We handle contracts with living artists.
Particular market you target: all
How often do you review work: year-round
Specific styles of work you prefer: comsumer products
We are: actively seeking new artists, seeking established artists through referral, reviewing unsolicited slides from fine artists, filing slides for possible future projects
Artists can contact us by: submitting portfolio for review by mail
Number of artists we work with presently: 10
We prefer to review: trannies, slides, CDs
Trade shows we attend: Surtex, ArtExpo, Licensing/NY and others

Art Licensing International Inc

Michael Woodward
1532 US 41 By Pass S #272, Venice, FL 34293
941/488-8464 941/488-8454 Fax
www.artlicensinginc.com <artlicensing@comcast.net>

Role in licensing industry: Licensing agents for artists, illustrators, photographers, concept designers as well as TV cartoon concepts. We basically handle collections of work submitted by artists which we aim to license across a range of product categories such as greeting cards, calendars, stationery and gift products, jigsaws, partyware, textiles, housewares, etc.
Needs: We require collections of art, illustrations or photography which have wide consumer appeal. CD presentations preferred but slides/transparencies and photocopies are acceptable. Style guide is preferred showing all the characters and a synopsis with story lines.
First contact and terms: Send examples on CD (tiff or jpg files), color photocopies or slides/transparencies with SASE. Fine artists should send short bio. Terms: 50/50 with no expenses to artist, as long as artist can provide high resolution scans if we agree on representation.
Tips: Look at actual products in retail outlets and get a feel for what is selling well. Ask store owners or sales assistants what is hot. Get to know the markets you are actually trying to sell your work into. Consider actual products when creating new art.

Alexandre A du M

Walter Mussienko
PO Box 34, Upper Marlborough, MD 20773
301/627-5170

We publish: giclées, limited editions, serigraphs
We review art: on an ongoing basis.
Number of living artists we work with: 4
Styles of artwork we publish: realism, impressionism
Our products are sold in: art galleries
We are: actively seeking new artists, seeking established artists through referral, reviewing unsolicited slides from fine artists, filing slides for possible future work
Artists can contact us by: submitting portfolio for review by mail
Best time of year to submit portfolio: Spring
We prefer to review: photos
We also distribute work from self-published artists.

American Greetings

PO Box 208, Sherman Center, OH 44274-0208

Applejack Art Partners

Michael Katz
PO Box 1528, Manchester Center, VT 05255-1527
800/362-3662 802/362-1082 Fax
www.applejackart.com

We publish: giclées, posters, limited editions
We also handle licensing for artists.
Styles of artwork we publish: wildlife, landscape
We are: actively seeking new artists, reviewing unsolicited slides from fine artists
We review art from fine artists: on a weekly basis
We have a review committee.
Artists can contact us by: submitting portfolio for review by mail
Best time of year to submit portfolio: year-round
We prefer to review: transparencies

Art Encounter

Brett Maly
3979 Spring Mountain Rd, Las Vegas, NV 89102-8613
702/227-0220
www.artencounter.com <rod@artencounter.com>

We publish: giclées, limited editions. We are also a gallery.
Number of living artists we work with: 5
Styles of artwork we publish: All
Our products are sold in: fine art galleries
We are: actively seeking new artists
We review art from fine artists: on a continual basis
We have a review committee.
Artists can contact us by: calling to arrange a personal interview to show portfolio, submitting portfolio for review by mail, or e-mailing portfolio
Best time of year to submit portfolio: year-round
We prefer to review: slides
Tips for those contacting us: phone, e-mail or simply send portfolio with SASE
We also distribute work from self-published artists.

Art in Motion

Jessica Gibson, Artist Relations
2000 Hartley Ave, Coquitlam, BC Canada V3K 6W5
800/663-1308 877/525-6166 Fax
www.artinmotion.com <jgibson@artinmotion.com>

We publish: posters
We also handle licensing for artists.
Our target market is: high-end retail stores; home decor, gift shops, galleries
Number of living artists we work with: 100+
Styles of artwork we publish: all images that have some commercial appeal
We are: actively seeking new artists
We review art from fine artists: on an ongoing basis; submissions are always welcome
We have a review committee.
Artists can contact us by: submitting portfolio for review by mail, e-mailing portfolio
Best time of year to submit portfolio: year-round
We prefer to review: color copies/photos/slides, e-mail jpgs, no originals please!
Tips for those contacting us: If artists are mailing submission, please indicate $0.00 commercial value for customs, or submission will unfortunately be refused.

Artful Greetings

Marian Whitterman
PO Box 52428, Durham, NC 27717
800/638-2733   919/598-8909 Fax
www.artfulgreetings.com   <myw@artfulgreetings.com>

We publish: greeting cards
Our target market is: card shops, gift shops, bookstores
Number of living artists we work with: 20
Styles of artwork we publish: multi-cultural
We are: actively seeking new artists
We review art from fine artists: year-round
We have a review committee.
Artists can contact us by: submitting portfolio for review by mail, e-mailing portfolio
Best time of year to submit portfolio: Jan - October
We prefer to review: transparency or photocopy

Avalanche Publishing

Cathy Hull
15262 Pipeline Ln, Huntington Beach, CA 92649
714/898-2400   714/898-2410 Fax
www.avalanchepub.com

We publish: calendars
We also handle licensing for artists.
Our target market is: bookstores, gift and mass market stores
Number of living artists we work with: 12
Styles of artwork we publish: decorative
We are: actively seeking new artists, seeking established artists through referral, reviewing unsolicited slides from fine artists
We review art from fine artists: as often as we need to; also at Surtex
We have a review committee.
Artists can contact us by: send samples first, then submit portfolio for review by mail
Best time of year to submit portfolio: year-round
We prefer to review: non-returnable
Tips for those contacting us: send non-returnable samples in the mail. We respond if interested.

Avanti Press

Photo Editor
6 W 18 St #12Fl, New York, NY 10011
212/414-1025   212/414-1055 Fax
www.avantipress.com   <artsubmissions@avantipress.com>

We publish: greeting cards
Our target market is: gift stores, card stores, supermarkets, etc.
Number of living artists we work with: 100s
Styles of artwork we publish: photographic only
We are: actively seeking new artists
We review art from fine artists: on a continual basis
We have a review committee.
Artists can contact us by: e-mailing portfolio
Best time of year to submit portfolio: ongoing
We prefer to review: low-resolution digital files
Tips for those contacting us: go to website for info

Bentley House Ltd

Jan Weiss
1410 Lesnick Ln, Walnut Creek, CA 94596-2737
925/935-5201   925/935-0213 Fax
www.bentleypublishinggroup.com
<jan@bentleypublishinggroup.com>

We publish: posters
We also handle licensing for artists.
Our target market is: chain stores, mass framers
Number of living artists we work with: 200
Styles of artwork we publish: large variety
We are: actively seeking new artists
We review art from fine artists: daily
We have a review committee.
Artists can contact us by: submitting portfolio for review by mail, e-mailing portfolio
Best time of year to submit portfolio: anytime
We prefer to review: slides, photos, jpgs
Tips for those contacting us: be patient, include a SASE

LICENSEES INCLUDING PUBLISHERS OF PRINTS, CALENDARS, GREETING CARDS, T-SHIRTS, ETC

Bill Goff Inc

Bill Goff
5 Bridge St, PO Box 977, Kent, CT 06757
860/927-1411   860/927-1987 Fax
www.goodsportsart.com   <bill.goff@snet.net>

We publish: prints, posters, limited editions, calendars
We also handle licensing for artists.
Styles of artwork we publish: sports
Our products are sold in: mail order, Internet
Number of living artists we work with: 8
We have a review committee.
We review art from fine artists: frequently
We are: reviewing unsolicited slides from fine artists
Artists can contact us by: submitting portfolio for review by mail, e-mailing portfolio
Best time of year to submit portfolio: anytime
We prefer to review: e-mail
Tips for those contacting us: sports art only

Billiard Library Company

Darian Baskin
1570 Seabright Ave, Long Beach, CA 90813-1131
562/437-5413   562/436-8817 Fax
www.billiardlibrary.com   <info@billiardlibrary.com>

We publish: posters and distribute prints
We also handle licensing for artists.
Our target market is: billiard suppliers and halls
Number of living artists we work with: 3
Styles of artwork we publish: billiard theme
We are: reviewing unsolicited slides from fine artists
We review art from fine artists: a few times a year
We have a review committee.
Artists can contact us by: submitting portfolio for review by mail, e-mailing portfolio
Best time of year to submit portfolio: early
We also distribute work from self-published artists.

Birds of a Feather Publishing

Mary Ericson
PO Box 100, Marshville, NC 28103
704/624-3576   704/624-2371 Fax
We publish: posters, limited editions, giclées
We also handle licensing for artists.
Our target market is: frame shops, art galleries
Number of living artists we work with: 2
Styles of artwork we publish: coastal

We are: reviewing unsolicited slides from fine artists, filing slides for possible future publication
We review art from fine artists: as they come in
We have a review committee.
Artists can contact us by: submitting portfolio for review by mail
We prefer to review: slides or photos
Tips for those contacting us: by mail only, provide a SASE for slides or prints
We also distribute work from self-published artists.

Bits and Pieces

Cindi Ziontz
214 Lincoln St 3205, Allston, MA 02134
617/254-3855 ext 107   617/779-9645 Fax
www.bitsandpieces.com   <cziontz@bitsandpieces.com>

We publish: prints, posters, serigraphs, limited editions, calendars, greeting cards
We also handle licensing for artists.
Styles of artwork we publish: various
Our products are sold in: direct mail catalog and web site
Number of living artists we work with: 30+
We have a review committee of three people.
We review art from fine artists: throughout the year
We are: actively seeking new artists
Artists can contact us by: submitting portfolio for review by mail, e-mailing portfolio
Best time of year to submit portfolio: Oct - May
Tips for those contacting us: send to art director. If we are in the middle of catalog production, it may take time to get a response.
We prefer to review: e-mail jpg files

Black River Publishing

Francis Nichols
PO Box 10091, Marina Del Rey, CA 90295-6091
310/694-0060
www.brpub.com

We publish: calendars
Our target market is: book stores and direct mail
Number of living artists we work with: 2
Styles of artwork we publish: varies
We are: filing slides for possible future publication
We review art from fine artists: when needed
We do not have a review committee.

Artists can contact us by: submitting portfolio for review by mail
Best time of year to submit portfolio: Spring and Summer
We prefer to review: photocopies or prints
Tips for those contacting us: no phone calls

Bradford Exchange
Kelly Ann Colgan
9333 N Milwaukee Ave, Niles, IL 60714
708/581-8205
www.bradfordexchange.com

Canadian Art Prints
Niki Krieger
6311 Westminster Hwy #110, Richmond, BC V7C 4V4 Canada
604/276-4551   604/276-4552 Fax
www.canadianartprints.com
<sales@canadianartprints.com

We publish: prints, posters, serigraphs, limited editions, calendars, greeting cards
We also handle licensing for artists.
Styles of artwork we publish: all
Our products are sold in: frame shops, gift stores, galleries
Number of living artists we work with: 100+
We have a review committee.
We review art from fine artists: every 4-6 weeks
We are: actively seeking new artists
Artists can contact us by: submitting portfolio for review by mail
Best time of year to submit portfolio: anytime
We prefer to review: slides, photos
Tips for those contacting us: include a breadth of imagery

Caravan International
Dale Byars
PO Box 768, Colleyville, TX 76034-0768
800/442-0036   800/894-6810 Fax
www.caravancards.com

We publish: greeting cards
We also handle licensing for artists.
Our products are sold in: museum gift shops
Number of living artists we work with: 20
We have a review committee.

We review art from fine artists: 3-4 times annually
We are: reviewing unsolicited slides from fine artists
Artists can contact us by: submitting portfolio for review by mail
Best time of year to submit portfolio: anytime
We prefer to review: slides, color copies

Carmel Fine Art
Louise Perrin, Carl
21 Stocker Rd, Verona, NJ 07044
973/571-1708   973-571-1768 Fax
ww.carmelprod.com   <carmelfineart@comcast.com>

We publish: posters, giclées, limited edtions and distrubte prints
Contact: Carl
We also handle licensing for artists.
Styles of artwork we publish: contemporary
Our products are sold in: various venues
We have a review committee.
We review art from fine artists: regulary
Number of living artists we work with: 11
We are: reviewing unsolicited slides from fine artists
Artists can contact us by: submitting portfolio for review by mail, e-mail portfolio
Best time of year to submit portfolio: anytime
We prefer to review: inexpensive samples

CBA/C Boyajian & Associates
C Boyajian
365 W Alameda Ave #308, Burbank, CA 91506
<cboyajian@pacbell.net>

We publish: serigraphs, limited editions, giclées
Styles of artwork we publish: varies
Our products are sold in: hotels, hospitality projects
We have a review committee.
We review art from fine artists: anytime
We are: seeking established artists through referral, reviewing unsolicited slides from fine artists, filing slides for possible future publication
Artists can contact us by: submitting portfolio for review by mail, e-mailing portfolio
Best time of year to submit portfolio: anytime
We prefer to review: transparencies
We also distribute work from self-published artists.

Chalk & Vermilion Fine Arts Inc

Eric Dannemann
55 Old Post Rd #2, Greenwich, CT 06830-6241
203/869-9500   203/869-9520 Fax
www.chalk-vermilion.com   <mail@chalk-vermilion.com>

We publish: posters, serigraphs, limited editions
Styles of artwork we publish: all
Our products are sold in: art galleries
We have a review committee.
We review art from fine artists: every month
We are: reviewing unsolicited slides from fine artists
Artists can contact us by: submitting portfolio for review by mail
We prefer to review: photos
Tips for those contacting us: send letter, slides, photos or reproductions of work, SASE

Collectible Art Publishing

May Allan
2044 Chestnut St, Philadelphia, PA 9103
215/629-8654   215/629-8611 Fax

We publish: posters, limited editions, greeting cards, distribute prints
Styles of artwork we publish: African-American
We are: actively seeking new artists, seeking established artists through referral, reviewing unsolicited slides from fine artists, filing slides for possible future publication
Artists can contact us by: calling to arrange a personal interview to show portfolio, submitting portfolio for review by mail, e-mailing portfolio
Best time of year to submit portfolio: anytime
We prefer to review: photos or mini-prints
We also distribute work from self-published artists.

Comstock Cards Inc

David Dela Crouix
600 S Rock Blvd #15, Reno, NV 89502-4115
702/856-9400   775/856-9406 Fax
www.comstockcards.com   <cindy@comstockcards.com>

We publish: greeting cards
Styles of artwork we publish: cartoons
Our products are sold in: Spencers, adult stores, lingerie stores
Number of living artists we work with: 37
We have a review committee.

We review art from illustrators.
We are: actively seeking new artists
Artists can contact us by: submitting portfolio for review by mail, e-mailing portfolio
Best time of year to submit portfolio: anytime
We prefer to review: line art
Tips for those contacting us: for return of samples send SASE

C R Gibson

Royce Hines
PO Box 14100, Nashville, TN 37214-1000

Creative Source Inc

Jan Anderson, Donna Richardson
115 W Main St, Greenville, KY 42345-1201
270/338-6958   270/338-7275 Fax
<csart@muhlon.com>

We publish: posters, limited editions, distribute prints
We also handle licensing for artists.
Styles of artwork we publish: all types
Our products are sold in: all types of stores
Number of living artists we work with: 8
We have a review committee.
We are: actively seeking new artists, seeking established artists through referral, filing slides for possible future publication
Artists can contact us by: submitting portfolio for review by mail, e-mailing portfolio
Best time of year to submit portfolio: anytime

Crockett Studios

A Broskie
PO Box 1543, Bennington, VT 05201
888/272-2158   888/272-2159 Fax
www.crockettstudios.com

We publish: serigraphs, limited editions, posters, greeting cards
We review art from fine artists: continuously
Our products are sold in: upscale gift stores
We are: actively seeking new artists
Artists can contact us by: submitting portfolio for review by mail
Best time of year to submit portfolio: December

De Montfort Fine Art Ltd

Helen Swaby
46-48 Mere Green Rd, Sutton Coldfield Birmingham
B7S S8T England
0044/121308-1129 0044/121323-2029 Fax
www.demontfortfineart.co.uk <info@demontfortfineart>

We publish: serigraphs, limited editions, giclées, print distributor
Styles of artwork we publish: contemporary
Number of living artists we work with: 70
We have a review committee.
We review art from fine artists: on a daily basis
We are: actively seeking new artists, reviewing unsolicited slides from fine artists,
Artists can contact us by: calling to arrange a personal interview to show portfolio, submitting portfolio for review by mail, e-mailing portfolio
Best time of year to submit portfolio: all year
We prefer to review: any format
Tips for those contacting us: Look at our web site; work needs to work well alongside existing range

Design Design

Tom Vituj
PO Box 2266, Grand Rapids, MI 49501-2266

E P Publishing

Evan Richmond
1939 S 300 W #144, Salt Lake City, UT 84115
801/274-8275 801/277-0397 Fax
www.ep-publishing.com
<erichmond@ep-publishing.com>

We publish: calendars
Our products are sold in: bookstores
We are: actively seeking new artists
Artists can contact us by: submitting portfolio for review by mail, e-mailing portfolio
Best time of year to submit portfolio: anytime

Everything Metal Imaginable Inc

Reneé Robbins
401 E Cypress, Visalia, CA 93277
800/777-8126 559/732-8126 559/732-5961 Fax
www.artbronze.com

Manufacture lost wax bronze sculpture

Fisher-Price

Henry Schmidt
636 Girard Ave, E Aurora, NY 14052
716/687-3983 716/687-5281 Fax

Manufacture toys. Need designers for label art.

Flying Colors

Joe McCormick
4117 W Jefferson Blvd, Los Angeles, CA 90016-4124
323/732-9994 323/731-0969 Fax
www.flying-colors.net <joe@flying-colors.net>

We publish: posters
We also handle licensing for artists.
Styles of artwork we publish: all except abstract
Our products are sold in: mass market and galleries
Number of living artists we work with: 25
We have a review committee.
We review art from fine artists: continuously
We are: actively seeking new artists, seeking established artists through referral, reviewing unsolicited slides from fine artists, filing slides for possible future publication
Artists can contact us by: calling to arrange a personal interview to show portfolio, submitting portfolio for review by mail, e-mailing portfolio
Best time of year to submit portfolio: January and July
We prefer to review: slides

Fotofolio

J Galant
561 Broadway, New York, NY 10012
212/226-0923 212/226-0072 Fax
www.fotofolio.com <jgalant@fotofolio.com>

We publish: posters, calendars, greeting cards, books, print distributor
We also handle licensing for artists.
Styles of artwork we publish: photography format
Our products are sold in: museum stores, bookstores, etc.
Number of living artists we work with: 300+
We have a review committee.
We review art from fine artists: regularly
We are: seeking established artists through referral
Artists can contact us by: see web site info for submitting works
We occasionally distribute work from self-published artists.

LICENSEES INCLUDING PUBLISHERS OF PRINTS, CALENDARS, GREETING CARDS, T-SHIRTS, ETC

Franklin Mint
Elizabeth Smith
RR 1, Media, PA 19091
www.franklinmint.com

Gartlan USA Inc
Robert Gartlan
560 Stokes Rd #23-397, Medford, NJ 08055
609/953-0207
www.gartlanusa.com <info@gartlanusa.com>

We publish: posters, limited editions, distribute prints
We also handle licensing for artists.
Styles of artwork we publish: realism
Our products are sold in: gift stores, collectibles, galleries
Number of living artists we work with: 4
We have a review committee.
We are: actively seeking new artists, seeking established artists through referral
Artists can contact us by: submitting portfolio for review by mail
Best time of year to submit portfolio: call

Glaspalast Editions
Peter Ulrich
Opeter Graten 5A, 86152 Augsburg, Germany
<phulrich@aol.com>

We publish: posters, serigraphs, books, distribute prints
We do not handle licensing for artists.
Our products are sold in: galleries
Number of living artists we work with: 30
We are: filing slides for possible future publication
Artists can contact us by: submitting portfolio for review by mail, e-mailing portfolio
Best time of year to submit portfolio: January and July

Golden Seal Art
Doug Ward
PO Box 55854, Seattle, WA 98155
206/533-0603   206/533-0702 Fax
www.goldensealart.com <doug@goldensealart.com>

We publish: prints, posters, serigraphs, limited editions, calendars, greeting cards, books, giclées, distribute prints
We also handle licensing for artists.
Styles of artwork we publish: see web site

Our products are sold in: traditional, corporate
Number of living artists we work with: 18
We have a review committee.
We review art from fine artists: quarterly or by invitation
We are: actively seeking new artists, seeking established artists through referral, filing slides for possible future publication
Artists can contact us by: submitting portfolio for review by mail, e-mailing portfolio, requesting submittal application
We prefer to review: 35mm slides
Tips for those contacting us: by phone, mail or e-mail

Haddads Fine Arts
Beth Hedstrom
3855 E Miraloma Ave, Anaheim, CA 92806-2124
714/996-2100   714/996-4153 Fax
www.haddadsfinearts.com

We publish: posters
We do not handle licensing for artists.
Styles of artwork we publish: everything
Our products are sold in: framing galleries, museums stores, etc.
Number of living artists we work with: 30
We have a review committee.
We review art from fine artists: year-round
We are: actively seeking new artists, reviewing unsolicited slides from fine artists
Artists can contact us by: submitting portfolio for review by mail (no e-mail!)
We prefer to review: slides or prints
Tips for those contacting us: need fresh, decorative approach. Look at art in chains.

Hadley House
Lisa Belak
11300 Hampshire Ave S, Bloomington, MN 55438
952/943-8474 952/943-8098 Fax
www.hadleyhouse.com <hadley@hadleyco.com>

We publish: prints, posters, limited editions, giclées, distributor
We also handle licensing for artists.
Styles of artwork we publish: realism is our main focus
Our products are sold in: mainly galleries and frame shops
Number of living artists we work with: 25

We have a review committee.

We review art from fine artists: every 6-8 weeks

We are: actively seeking new artists, reviewing unsolicited slides from fine artists

Artists can contact us by: submitting portfolio for review by mail

Best time of year to submit portfolio: all year

We prefer to review: slides

Tips for those contacting us: include bio, slides and any other pertinent info

We also distribute work from self-published artists.

Hallmark
Carol King
PO Box 419580, Kansas City, MO 64141-8400

Hamilton Collection Inc
Jennifer Cope
4810, Executive Park Ct, Jacksonville, FL 32216-6069
904/723-6000
www.hamiltoncollection.com

Hasbro
Cathy Meredith, VP of Licensing and PR
1027 Newport Ave, Pawtucket, RI 02862
401/727-5808   401/727-5595 Fax
www.hasbrotoy.com

Image Maker Enterprises
Bud Katich
12348 W Ginger Creek Dr, Boise, ID 83713
208/378-4417   208/323-6130 Fax
www.imagemaker.org   <bkatich@imagemaker.org>

We publish: limited editions, giclées, greeting cards, distribute prints

We also handle licensing for artists.

Styles of artwork we publish: all

Number of living artists we work with: 15

We have a review committee.

We are: actively seeking new artists, seeking established artists through referral, reviewing unsolicited slides from fine artists

Artists can contact us by: submitting portfolio for review by mail, e-mailing portfolio

Imlay Designs
Nancy Imlay
5609 W 6th Ave, Lakewood, CO 80214
303/232-8200   303/232-8204 Fax
www.imlaydesigns.com   <nancy@imlaydesigns.com>

We publish: giclée prints

Styles of artwork we publish: all

Our products are sold in: we sell to commercial industry

Number of living artists we work with: 10

We have a review committee.

We review art from fine artists: once a month

We are: actively seeking new artists, seeking established artists through referral, reviewing unsolicited slides from fine artists, filing slides for possible future publication

Artists can contact us by: submitting portfolio for review by mail, e-mailing portfolio

Indigo Gallery
Wendy Foster
163 W Mountain Ave, Ft Collins, CO 80524
<indigo@frii.com>

We publish: giclée prints, distribute prints

We do not handle licensing for artists.

Our products are sold in: art galleries

We review art from fine artists: twice a month

We are: actively seeking new artists

Artists can contact us by: e-mailing portfolio

Tips for those contacting us: Be brief with a few good visuals.

Inspirations Unlimited
John
PO Box 5097, Crestline, CA 92325
909/338-6758 909/338-2907 Fax

We publish: greeting cards

We do not handle licensing for artists.

Our products are sold in: all types of places

Number of living artists we work with: 22

We are: reviewing unsolicited slides from fine artists

We prefer to review: color copies of your artwork with return envelope

J Stone Cards Inc

1 J Stone Plz, Silverton, OR 97381
503/873-7298
www.jstonecards.com <jstonecards@aol.com>

We publish: greeting cards
We do not handle licensing for artists.
Styles of artwork we publish: black and white, fine line, illustrators
Our products are sold in: very high-end museum stores
Number of living artists we work with: 4
We do not have a review committee.
We review art from fine artists: quarterly
We are: seeking established artists through referral
Artists can contact us by: submitting portfolio for review by mail, e-mailing portfolio
Best time of year to submit portfolio: anytime
We prefer to review: photos
Tips for those contacting us: Know the J Stone line

Joan Cawley Gallery Ltd

Ray Granger
1410 W 14th St #101, Tempe, AZ 85281-6909
800/835-0075   480/858-0363 Fax
www.jcgltd.com <rayg@jcgltd.com>

We publish: posters, limited editions
We also handle licensing for artists.
Styles of artwork we publish: Southwest, landscape
Our products are sold in: art galleries, interior decorators, furniture stores
Number of living artists we work with: 60+
We have a review committee.
We review art from fine artists: Spring and Fall
We are: actively seeking new artists, reviewing unsolicited slides from fine artists
Artists can contact us by: calling to arrange a personal interview to show portfolio, submitting portfolio for review by mail (no slides, please)
Best time of year to submit portfolio: February and April
We prefer to review: photos
Tips for those contacting us: Send photos, portfolio and SASE. Don't send originals. Portfolio should include bio.
We also distribute work from self-published artists.

Lang Companies

Yvonne Groenvelt
514 Wells St, Delafield, WI 53018
262/646-3399

We publish: calendars, greeting card, books
Styles: country-oriented (no abstract or extremely contemporary styles)
Our products are sold in: gift shops, bookstores
We have a review committee.
We review art from fine artists: all year
We are: reviewing unsolicited slides from fine artists
Artists can contact us by: submitting portfolio for review by mail
Best time of year to submit portfolio: all year
We prefer to review: color copies, photos, slides
Tips for those contacting us: call or write for artist guidelines

Leanin' Tree

Edward Trumble
6055 Longbow Dr, Boulder, CO 80301-3296

LPG Greetings Inc

Judy Cecchi
4000 Porett Dr, Gurnee, IL 60031
847/244-4414   847/244-0188 Fax
www.lpggreetings.com

We publish: Christmas cards
We do not handle licensing for artists.
Styles of artwork we publish: Christmas
Our products are sold in: gift, department and discount stores
Number of living artists we work with: 50-70
We have a review committee.
We review art from fine artists: annually
We are: actively seeking new artists, seeking established artists through referral, reviewing unsolicited slides from fine artists
Artists can contact us by: submitting portfolio for review by mail
Best time of year to submit portfolio: January - February
We prefer to review: color copies
Tips for those contacting us: Do not e-mail your portfolio; it will be refused.
We also distribute work from self-published artists.

Lesli Art Inc
Stan Shevrin
20558 Chatsboro, Woodland Hills, CA 91364
818/999-9228   818/999-0833 Fax
www.lesliart.com   <artlesli@aol.com>

We publish: posters, limited editions, giclées
We also handle licensing for artists.
Our products are sold in: art galleries
We have a review committee.
We review art from fine artists: at all times
We are: actively seeking new artists, seeking established artists through referral, reviewing unsolicited slides from fine artists, filing slides for possible future publication
Artists can contact us by: submitting portfolio for review by mail, e-mailing portfolio
Best time of year to submit portfolio: year-round
We prefer to review: 4x6″ photos or slides
Tips for those contacting us: send quality images

Life Greetings
Kathy Brennan
PO Box 468, Little Compton, RI 02837
401/635-8535   401/635-4918 Fax

We publish: greeting cards
We do not handle licensing for artists.
Styles of artwork we publish: pen and ink
Our products are sold in: Christian supply stores
Number of living artists we work with: many
We do not have a review committee.
We review art from fine artists: when submitted
We are: actively seeking new artists
Artists can contact us by: submitting portfolio for review by mail
Best time of year to submit portfolio: anytime
We prefer to review: photocopies

Maid in the Shade
Laird Ehlert
PO Box 341, Church St Station, New York, NY 10008
201/659-1269   212/962-1420 Fax
www.maidintheshade.com   <Laird18@hotmail.com>

We publish: greeting cards
We do not handle licensing for artists.
Styles of artwork we publish: humorous, alternative

Our products are sold in: alternative shops, gay bookstores
Number of living artists we work with: 5
We do not have a review committee.
We review art from fine artists: as time allows
We are: not seeking artists at this time
Artists can contact us by: submitting portfolio for review by mail, e-mailing portfolio
Best time of year to submit portfolio: anytime
We prefer to review: photocopies or electronic

Main Floor Editions
Liz
4943 McConnell Ave #W, Los Angeles, CA 90066-6713
800/717-1222   310/823-4399 Fax

We publish: posters
We also handle licensing for artists.
Styles of artwork we publish: decorative
Our products are sold in: mass market, retail
Number of living artists we work with: 70
We have a review committee.
We review art from fine artists: all the time
We are: actively seeking new artists
Artists can contact us by: submitting portfolio for review by mail
We prefer to review: color copies, pictures
We also distribute work from self-published artists.

Marcel Schurman
Dion Puhl
2500 N Watney Wy, Fairfield, CA 94533-6724

Marian Heath
Molly Del Mastro
PO Box 3130, Waeham, MA 02571-3130

Mixed Blessings
Elise Okrend
PO Box 97212, Raleigh, NC 27624-7212
919/847-7944   919/847-6429 Fax
www.mixedblessings.com   <mixbless@aol.com>

We publish: greeting cards
We do not handle licensing for artists.

Our products are sold in: greeting card stores, department stores
Number of living artists we work with: 10
We have a review committee.
We review art from fine artists: twice a year
We are: actively seeking new artists
Artists can contact us by: submitting portfolio for review by mail, e-mailing portfolio
Best time of year to submit portfolio: fall and winter
We prefer to review: color photocopies
Tips for those contacting us: Send or e-mail samples. We will contact you if interested.
We also distribute work from self-published artists.

Mother Tongue Ink
Meghan Garrity
37010 SE Snuffic Rd, Estacada, OR 97023
503/630-7848   503/630-7048 Fax
www.wemoon.ws   <matrix@wemoon.ws>

We publish: calendars, greeting cards
We do not handle licensing for artists.
Styles of artwork we publish: We only publish art created by women.
Our products are sold in: women's bookstores, co-ops, New Age stores
Number of living artists we work with: 150
We have a review committee.
We review art from fine artists: annually
We are: actively seeking new artists, seeking established artists through referrals
Best time of year to submit portfolio: summertime
We prefer to review: high-quality photos
Tips for those contacting us: Send SASE for submission and release information. Do not send artwork without a release form.
We also distribute work from self-published artists.

Mr. City Cards
Kurt Fulton
PO Box 958, New York, NY 10013
212/941-8563   212/629-5752 Fax
www.saintcards.com/MrCityCards
<MrCityCards@saintcards.com>

We publish: greeting cards
We do not handle licensing for artists.

Styles of artwork we publish: contemporary fine art and illustration
Our products are sold in: museum shops to specialty gift stores
Number of living artists we work with: 14
We do not have a review committee.
We review art from fine artists: continuously
We are: actively seeking new artists, reviewing unsolicited slides from fine artists
Artists can contact us by: submitting portfolio for review by mail, e-mailing portfolio

Museum Editions
Charles Daley
32 Relyea Pl #2, New Rochelle, NY 10801-6910
914/654-9370   914/654-0622 Fax
www.fazzino.com

We publish: posters, serigraphs, limited editions, books
We also handle licensing for artists.
Styles of artwork we publish: animation
Our products are sold in: art galleries
We have a review committee.
We are: reviewing unsolicited slides from fine artists
Artists can contact us by: submitting portfolio for review by mail
Best time of year to submit portfolio: Summer
Tips for those contacting us: call after 12:00PM ET

New Era Publishing
Nick Nichols
2324 Ridgepoint Dr #D, Austin, TX 78754
512/928-3200   512/928-3053 Fax
www.newerapublishing.com
<info@newerapublishing.com>

We publish: giclées
We also handle licensing for artists.
Our products are sold to: corporations
Number of living artists we work with: 21
We have a review committee.
We review art from fine artists: once a month
We are: reviewing unsolicited slides from fine artists
Artists can contact us by: submitting portfolio for review by mail, e-mailing portfolio
Tips for those contacting us: Please allow four to six weeks for review and always provide SASE.

New York Graphic Society
Richard Fleischmann
129 Glover Ave, Norwalk, CT 06850
800/677-6947   203/846-2105 Fax

We publish: posters
Styles of artwork we publish: open
Our products are sold in: picture galleries, home decor showrooms
Number of living artists we work with: 500
We have a review committee.
We review art from fine artists: continually
We are: actively seeking new artists, seeking established artists through referral, reviewing unsolicited slides from fine artists
Artists can contact us by: calling to arrange a personal interview to show portfolio, submitting portfolio for review by mail, e-mailing portfolio
Best time of year to submit portfolio: open

Next Monet Inc
444 Townsend St, San Francisco, CA 94107
888/914-5050

Direct mail marketing; publishers of high-end giclées.

Nobleworks
Ron
PO Box 1275, Hoboken, NJ 07030-1275
201/420-0095   201/420-0079 Fax
www.nobleworksinc.com   <rkanfi@nobleworksinc.com>

We publish: greeting cards
We also handle licensing for artists.
Styles of artwork we publish: hip
Our products are sold in: card stores and bookstores
Number of living artists we work with: 100
We do not have a review committee.
We review art from fine artists: regularly
We are: reviewing unsolicited slides from fine artists
We prefer to review: prints or via e-mail

Novo Card Publishers Inc
Peter Eiden and Jill Sndyer
3630 W Pratt Ave, Lincolnwood, IL 60712
847/763-0077   847/763-0072 Fax
www.novocard.net   <art@novocard.net

We publish: greeting cards
Person in charge of selecting art: art department
We do not handle licensing for artists.
Styles of artwork we publish: conservative
Number of living artists we work with: 10 per year
We do not have a review committee.
We review art from fine artists: twice a year
We are: actively seeking new artists
Artists can contact us by: submitting portfolio for review by mail, e-mailing portfolio
Best time of year to submit portfolio: Winter and Summer
We prefer to review: ones that are eye-catching
Tips for those contacting us: e-mail or fax, don't call

Oatmeal Studios
Helene Lehrer
PO Box 138, Rochester, VT 05767
802/767-3171   802/767-9890
<helene@oatmealstudios.com>

We publish: greeting cards
We also handle licensing for artists.
Styles of artwork we publish: fun character illustrations
Our products are sold: wherever greeting cards are sold
Number of living artists we work with: 15
We have a review committee.
We review art from fine artists: within 6-8 weeks of receipt
We are: actively seeking new artists
Artists can contact us by: submitting portfolio for review by mail
Best time of year to submit portfolio: anytime
We prefer to review: color or B&W photocopies
Tips for those contacting us: write for our guidelines
We also distribute work from self-published artists.

Ontario Federation of Anglers and Hunters
Deborah Carew
PO Box 2800, Peterborough, Ontario Canada K9J 8L5
705/748-6324   705/748-9577 Fax
www.ofah.org   <ofah@ofah.org>

We publish: greeting cards, limited editions, calendars
Person in charge of selecting art: varies according to project

We review art: anytime but specifically May deadline for yearly calendar contest

We have a review committee.

Styles of artwork we publish: wildlife, realistic

Number of living artists we work with: varies

We are: actively seeking new artists, reviewing unsolicited work from fine artists, filing slides for pssible future work

Artists can contact us by: submitting portfolio for review by mail, e-mailing portfolio, entering calendar contest

Best time of year to submit portfolio: Spring

We prefer to review: any; no originals

Tips for those contacting us: Look at your work objectively and consider whether it fits the wildlife market.

Optima International Art Prints

Antonio Domenech

C/Comalaoa, 3, Barcelona, Spain 08032

934/553763   934/368058 Fax

www.optimaintec.com   <info@optimaintec.com>

We publish: prints, posters

We also handle licensing for artists.

Styles of artwork we publish: all kinds

Our products are sold in: furniture stores

Number of living artists we work with: 15

We have a review committee.

We review art from fine artists: every month

We are: reviewing unsolicited slides from fine artists

Artists can contact us by: calling to arrange a personal interview to show portfolio, submitting portfolio for review by mail, e-mailing portfolio

---

Papertrail Press

Irene McGill

3060 Kerner Blvd #K, San Rafael, CA 94901

415/458-3515   415/458-3518 Fax

www.papertrailpress.com   <imcgi@aol.com>

We publish: greeting cards

We also handle licensing for artists.

Styles of artwork we publish: humorous illustrations of women

Our products are sold in: boutiques, gift shops, department stores

Number of living artists we work with: 4

We do not have a review committee.

We review art from fine artists: upon receipt

We are: actively seeking new artists, seeking established artists through referral

Artists can contact us by: submitting portfolio for review by mail

Best time of year to submit portfolio: Nov - Dec

We prefer to review: color copies

Paramount Press Inc

Jerry Seymour

PO Box 156, Asheville, NY 14710-0156

716/763-1744   800/647-2901 Fax

www.paramountpress.com   <ppi@madbbs.com>

We publish: limited editions, greeting cards, giclées, print distributor, books

We do not handle licensing for artists.

Styles of artwork we publish: galleries, bookstores

Our products are sold in: historical

Number of living artists we work with: 4

We do not have a review committee.

We review art from fine artists: as they arrive

We are: actively seeking new artists

Artists can contact us by: calling to arrange a personal interview to show portfolio, submitting portfolio for review by mail

Best time of year to submit portfolio: January - March

We also distribute work from self-published artists: depends on quality

---

Photo/Chronicles

David Deitch

PO Box 383, New York, NY 10113-0383

718/765-1566

We publish: posters, greeting cards

We also handle licensing for artists.

Styles of artwork we publish: photography

Our products are sold in: museum shops, bookstores

Number of living artists we work with: 200+

We do not have a review committee.

We review art from fine artists: constantly

We are: actively seeking new artists

Artists can contact us by: calling to arrange a personal interview to show portfolio

Best time of year to submit portfolio: anytime

Tips for those contacting us: Must telephone before submitting anything

Porter Design

Mary Porter
38 Anacapa St, Santa Barbara, CA 93101
805/568-5433   805/568-5435 Fax

We publish: posters, limited editions, greeting cards, print distributor
We have a review committee.
We review art from fine artists: continuously
We do not handle licensing for artists.
Styles of artwork we publish: mostly 16th - 19th century decorative
Our products are sold in: interior designers, gift stores, galleries
Number of living artists we work with: 5
We have a review committee.
We are: reviewing unsolicited slides from fine artists
Artists can contact us by: submitting portfolio for review by mail
Best time of year to submit portfolio: Dec and May
We prefer to review: transparencies or photocopies

Poster Porters

Mark Simard
PO Box 9241, Seattle, WA 98109
206/286-0818 206/286-0820 Fax
www.posterporters.com <posterporters@compuserve.com>

We publish: posters
We also handle licensing for artists.
Styles of artwork we publish: landscapes, seascapes
Our products are sold: galleries, craft stores, museums, gift stores
Number of living artists we work with: 11
We have a review committee.
We review art from fine artists: all the time
We are: actively seeking new artists, reviewing unsolicited work from fine artists
Artists can contact us by: submitting portfolio for review by mail, e-mailing portfolio
We also distribute work from self-published artists.

Poster Service

Steven L Garner
10305 Rading Rd, Cincinnati, OH 45241
513/577-7100 513/577-7110 Fax
www.posterservice.com <sgarner@posterservice.com>

We publish: prints, poster
We also handle licensing for artists.
We have a review committee.
We are: actively seeking new artists
Artists can contact us by: e-mailing portfolio
Best time of year to submit portfolio: September
We prefer to review: color copies

Posters International

Karen
1200 Castlefield Ave, Toronto, Ontario Canada
416/789-7156   416/789-7159 Fax

We publish: posters
We do not handle licensing for artists.
Styles of artwork we publish: varies
Our products are sold in: design-oriented stores
Number of living artists we work with: 25
We have a review committee.
We review art from fine artists: on an ongoing basis
Artists can contact us by: submitting portfolio for review by mail
Best time of year to submit portfolio: April - May
We prefer to review: slides or photos

Progressive Editions

Michael Havers
37 Sherbourne St, Toronto, Ontario Canada
416/860-0983 416/367-2724
www.progressiveeditions.com
<info@progressiveeditions.com>

We publish: serigraphs
We also handle licensing for artists.
Styles of artwork we publish: contemporary
Our products are sold in: retail galleries
Number of living artists we work with: 77
We do not have a review committee.
We review art from fine artists: once a month
We are: actively seeking new artists, reviewing unsolicited slides from fine artists
Artists can contact us by: calling to arrange a personal interview to show portfolio, submitting portfolio for review by mail, e-mailing portfolio
Best time of year to submit portfolio: anytime
Tips for those contacting us: submit only recent work

Ravensburger
www.ravensburger.com

Raymond Greenberg Art Publishing
Ray Greenberg
42 Leone Ln, Chester, NY 10918
825/469-6699   845/469-5955 Fax
www.raymondlgreenberg.com

We publish: posters
We also handle licensing for artists.
Styles of artwork we publish: figurative, still life
Our products are sold in: mass market, galleries
Number of living artists we work with: 20
We do not have a review committee.
We review art from fine artists: regularly
We are: actively seeking new artists, seeking established artists through referral, reviewing unsolicited slides from fine artists
Artists can contact us by: submitting portfolio for review by mail
Best time of year to submit portfolio: Summer
We prefer to review: prints, slides

Reco International Corp
Box 951, 138 Haven Ave, Port Washington, NY 11050
516/767-2400 516/767-2409 Fax
www.reco.com   <recoint@aol.com>

Recycled Paper Products
Melinda Gordon
3636 N Broadway St, Chicago, IL 60613-4488

Red Farm Studios
Lisa Saundrez
PO Box 347, Pawtucket, RI 02862-0347

Red Oak Publishers
Ellis Felker
14872 Creek Ln, Muscoda, WI 53573
800/601-8893   888/264-3156 Fax
www.redoakcards.com   <redoak@mwt.net

We publish: posters, greeting cards
We do not handle licensing for artists.

Styles of artwork we publish: photos, art
Our products are sold in: gift shops, bookstores, etc.
Number of living artists we work with: 10
We have a review committee.
We review art from fine artists: every 8-10 months
We are: actively seeking new artists, reviewing unsolicited slides from fine artists
Artists can contact us by: submitting portfolio for review by mail
Best time of year to submit portfolio: anytime

Richardson Gallery
Mark Richardson
3670 S Virginia St, Reno, NV 89502-6015
702/828-0888   775/828-4329
www.richardsonfineart.com   <fineart@intercomm.com>

We publish: giclées, limited editions
We do not handle licensing for artists.
Styles of artwork we publish: open to all
Our products are sold in: fine art galleries
Number of living artists we work with: 77
We do not have a review committee.
We review art from fine artists: regularly
We are: seeking established artists through referral
Artists can contact us by: submitting portfolio for review by mail, e-mailing portfolio
Best time of year to submit portfolio: anytime
We prefer to review: prints

Rockshots Greeting Cards
Bob Vesce
20 Vandam St #4Fl, New York, NY 10013-1274
212/243-9661   212/604-9060 Fax

We publish: calendars, greeting cards
We do not handle licensing for artists.
Styles of artwork we publish: cartoon, adult
Our products are sold in: department stores, card and gift stores, specialty shops
Number of living artists we work with: varies
We do not have a review committee.
We review art from fine artists: anytime
We are: actively seeking new artists, seeking established artists through referral
Artists can contact us by: submitting photocopied samples for review by mail

Best time of year to submit portfolio: anytime
We prefer to review: color photocopies
We also distribute work from self-published artists.

SE Feinman Fine Arts Ltd
Stephen Feinman
448 Broome St, New York, NY 10013-2608
212/431-6820

We publish: limited editions, print distributor
We do not handle licensing for artists.
Styles of artwork we publish: all
Our products are sold in: galleries
Number of living artists we work with: 4
We do not have a review committee.
We are: actively seeking new artists, reviewing unsolicited slides from fine artists
Artists can contact us by: submitting portfolio for review by mail
Best time of year to submit portfolio: all year
We also distribute work from self-published artists.

Schiftan Inc
Harvey Cohen
1300 Steel Rd W #4, Morrisville, PA 19067
215/428-2900   215/295-2345
www.schiftan.net   <schiftan@erols.com>

We publish: prints, posters
We also handle licensing for artists.
Our products are sold in: furniture stores, specialty shops, department stores
Number of living artists we work with: 20
Best time of year to submit portfolio: anytime

Shades of Color
Adrian Woods
PO Box 5523, Gardena, CA 90249
www.shadescalendars.com   <shades@shades.com>

We publish: calendars
We do not handle licensing for artists.
Styles of artwork we publish: African-American
Our products are sold in: galleries, bookstores, gift shops
Number of living artists we work with: 6
We do not have a review committee.

We review art from fine artists: annually
Artists can contact us by: submitting portfolio for review by mail, e-mailing portfolio
Best time of year to submit portfolio: Aug-Sept
We also distribute work from self-published artists.

Sole Source Inc
M Donnelly
63820 Clausen Dr, Bend, OR 97701
541/389-0360   541/389-0642 Fax
<art@sole-source.com>

We publish: greeting cards
We review art from fine artists: every quarter
Number of living artists we work with: 20
Styles of artwork we publish: animals (pets), flowers, trucks, heavy equipment, line art for foil, watercolors, mixed media, B&W
We are: actively seeking new artists, reviewing unsolicited work from fine artists
Artists can contact us by: e-mailing their portoflio

Sourire
Marlene Reed
PO Box 159, Old Chelsea Station, New York, NY 10011
718/573-4624
www.cardsorbust.com   <admin@cardsorbust.com>

We publish: greeting cards
We review art from fine artists: periodically
We also handle licensing for artists.
Our products are sold in: gift shops, stationery stores
Number of living artists we work with: 5
We are: actively seeking new artists
Artists can contact us by: sending SASE for guidelines
Number of artists we work with presently: 25
Tips for those contacting us: follow guidelines posted at our web site
Best time of year to submit portfolio: year-round
We prefer to review: cards or photocopies

LICENSEES INCLUDING PUBLISHERS OF PRINTS, CALENDARS, GREETING CARDS, T-SHIRTS, ETC

Sports Spectrum

Pat Fox
324 S Pacific Coast Hwy #201, Redondo Beach, CA 90277
800/752-9426   310/543-0503
www.sportsgreetingcards.com   <sportsspect@aol.com>

We publish: greeting cards
We also handle licensing for artists.
Styles of artwork we publish: varies
Number of living artists we work with: 5
We have a review committee.
We review art from fine artists: every month
We are: actively seeking new artists
Artists can contact us by: e-mailing portfolio
Best time of year to submit portfolio: anytime
We prefer to review: any time
We also distribute work from self-published artists.

Studio Chevalier

James Miller
60 Borden St, Shrewsbury, NJ 07702
732/741-9323   732/741-9312 Fax

We publish: stationery, imprintables
We do not handle licensing for artists.
Styles of artwork we publish: engraved
Our products are sold in: high-end stationery shops
Number of living artists we work with: 4
We have a review committee.
We review art from fine artists: ongoing
We are: actively seeking new artists, reviewing unsolicited slides from fine artists
Artists can contact us by: submitting portfolio for review by mail
Best time of year to submit portfolio: anytime

Tom Binder Fine Arts

Tom Binder
4027 Lincoln Blvd, Marina del Rey, CA 90292-5613
310/822-1080   310/822-1580 Fax
www.artman.net   <info@artman.net>

We publish: limited editions, print distributor
We also handle licensing for artists.
Styles of artwork we publish: varies
Our products are sold in: graphic stores
Number of living artists we work with: 3
We are: filing slides for possible future publication
Artists can contact us by: submitting portfolio for review by mail
Best time of year to submit portfolio: anytime
We prefer to review: non-returnable formats

UC Productions

Sofia Stambolieva
101 W 23 St #2715, New York, NY 10011
718/375-0306
www.ucproductions.com   <info@ucproductions.com>

Unique Greetings Inc

Mike Norman
PO Box 5783, Manchester, NH 03108-5783

We publish: prints, posters, greeting cards, books
We also handle licensing for artists.
Styles of artwork we publish: all
Our products are sold in: gift shops, supermarkets
Number of living artists we work with: 12
We have a review committee.
We review art from fine artists: year-round
We are: actively seeking new artists, reviewing unsolicited slides from fine artists,
Artists can contact us by: submitting portfolio for review by mail
Best time of year to submit portfolio: anytime
We prefer to review: any
Tips for those contacting us: send a SASE
We also distribute work from self-published artists.

Universe Art and Image

Galina Ivanov
25577 Detroit Rd, Westlake, OH 44145
440/934-1167   440/892-4084 Fax
<galina@century.net>

We publish: giclées
We do not handle licensing for artists.
Our products are sold in: art galleries
Number of living artists we work with: 42
We do not have a review committee.
We review art from fine artists: once a month
We are: actively seeking new artists, seeking established artists through referral
Artists can contact us by: submitting portfolio for review by mail
Best time of year to submit portfolio: anytime
We also distribute work from self-published artists.

Wild Apple Graphics

Nancy Dunwell
526 Woodstock Rd, Woodstock, VT 05091-7702
802/457-3003   802/457-5891 Fax
www.wildapple.com   <nancy.dunwell@wildapple.com>

We publish: posters, distribute prints
We also handle licensing for artists.
Styles of artwork we publish: view the web site to see our styles
Our products are sold in: Pier 1, Z Gallerie, Bombay, BB+B, etc
We have a review committee.
We review art from fine artists: 2-3 times per month
We are: actively seeking new artists, seeking established artists through referral, reviewing unsolicited slides from fine artists, filing slides for possible future publication
Artists can contact us by: submitting portfolio for review by mail, e-mailing portfolio
Best time of year to submit portfolio: all year long
Tips for those contacting us: see our web site for directions

Winn Devon Art Group

Karen Schweitzer
PO Box 80096, 6015 6th Ave S, Seattle, WA 98108
206/763-9544   206/762-1389 Fax
www.winndevon.com   <kschweitzer@winndevon.com>

We publish: prints, posters, serigraphs, limited editions, giclées
We also handle licensing for artists.
Styles of artwork we publish: decorative, variety
Our products are sold in: furniture stores, galleries, custom frame shops
Number of living artists we work with: 100+
We have a review committee.
We review art from fine artists: ongoing basis
We are: actively seeking new artists
Artists can contact us by: submitting portfolio for review by mail, e-mailing portfolio
We prefer to review: any kind is fine

WHOLESALE ART SALES

Picture Source

Diana Sharon
5961 Corson Ave S, Seattle, WA 98108
800/345-5973   206/767-2427
www.picture.source.com   <dsharon@picture-source.com>
We are a print distributor
We sell to the trade.
We do not have a review committee.
We are: actively seeking new prints to sell
Artists can contact us by: submitting portfolio for review by mail, e-mailing portfolio
Best time of year to submit portfolio: anytime
We prefer to review: prints, computer files
Tips for those contacting us: e-mail is best

Aaims Publishers

Angela Malik
PO Box 241777, Los Angeles, CA 90024-0577
213/968-1105
<aaimspub@aol.com>

We publish: books
Styles of fine art we tend to need: open to all
Our target market is: book cover design

A & B Distributors

Maxwell Taylor
PO Box 340, Flagstaff, AZ 86002-0340
800/523-2053 520/526-1967 Fax

We publish: books
We are: actively seeking illustrators
Artists can contact us by: submitting portfolio for review by mail
Best time of year to submit portfolio: September
Tips for those contacting us: include resumé

Art Direction Books Inc

Kevin Lopez
456 Glenbrook Rd, Glenbrook, CT 06906
203/353-1441   203/353-1371 Fax

We publish: books, art
Contact person: Don Barron
Styles of fine art we tend to need: commercial advertising
Our target market is: art directors, designers
Types of artwork you hire free-lancers for: cover art
We are: actively seeking illustrators
Artists can contact us by: calling to arrange a personal interview to show portfolio
Best time of year to submit portfolio: anytime
We prefer to review: photoprints

Bandanna Books

Brian Newborn
319-B Anacampa St, Santa Barbara, CA 93101
805/584-3559 Fax
www.bandannabooks.com <sasha@bandannabooks.com>

We publish: books
Contact person: Sasha Newborn
Styles of fine art we tend to need: cover art and B&W book illustration
Our target market is: universities
We are: actively seeking illustrators
Artists can contact us by: submitting a non-returnable portfolio for review by mail
Best time of year to submit portfolio: all year
We prefer to review: photoprints
Tips for those contacting us: if we think your art will fit a cover, then we will consider it and call you

Cartwheel Books/Scholastic Inc

Edie Weinberg
557 Broadway, New York, NY 10012
212/343-4404 212/343-6620 Fax
www.scholastic.com   <eweinberg@scholastic.com>

We publish: books
Contact person: editorial
Styles of fine art we tend to need: wide variety
Our target market is: bookstores, mass merchandisers
Types of artwork you hire free-lancers for: illustrating all our books
We are: actively seeking fine artists, actively seeking illustrators, seeking artists through referral, reviewing unsolicited work from fine artists, filing slides for possible future work
Artists can contact us by: calling to arrange a personal interview to show portfolio
We prefer to review: photoprints
Tips for those contacting us: young and bright, graphic and colorful

Fort Ross Inc

Dr Vladimir Kartsu
26 Arthur Pl, Yonkers, NY 10707
914/375-6448   914/375-6439 Fax
<ftross@ix.netcom.com>

We publish: books
Styles of fine art we tend to need: realistic, romance,
sci-fi, fantasy
Our target market is: Europe
We are: actively seeking illustrators, reviewing unsolicited
work from fine artists, filing slides for possible future work
Artists can contact us by: submitting portfolio for review
by mail
We prefer to review: photoprints
Tips for those contacting us: attention to detail

Gayot Publications

Walter Mladina
6006 Wilshire Blvd, Los Angeles, CA 90036
323/965-3529
www.gayot.com   <info@gayot.com>

We publish: books
Our target market is: travelers, restaurants
Types of artwork you hire free-lancers for: photos
We are: filing slides for possible future work
Artists can contact us by: submitting portfolio for review by
mail
We prefer to review: bio

The Graduate Group

Mara Whitman
PO Box 370351, West Hartford, CT 06137-0351
860/233-2330
www.graduategroup.com   <graduategroup@hotmail.com>

We publish: books
Our target market is: libraries, bookstores
Types of artwork you hire free-lancers for: book covers
We are: reviewing unsolicited work from fine artists
Artists can contact us by: submitting portfolio for review by
mail, e-mailing portfolio
Best time of year to submit portfolio: anytime
We prefer to review: bio

Judson Press

Wendy Ronga
588 N Gulph Rd, King of Prussia, PA 19406
610/768-2223   610/768-2441 Fax
<wendy.ronga@abc-usa.org>

We publish: books
Styles of fine art we tend to need: varies depending on the
project or theme
Our target market is: Christians, educators, children
Types of artwork you hire free-lancers for: cover art
We hire: illustrators, designers, photographers
We are: actively seeking illustrators, reviewing unsolicited
work from fine artists, filing slides for possible future work
Artists can contact us by: submitting portfolio for review
by mail, e-mailing portfolio
Best time of year to submit portfolio: anytime
We prefer to review: photoprints
Tips for those contacting us: A good presentation is really
important. I look for concept artists and people who draw
people well.

Loompanics Unlimited

Gia Cosindas
PO Box 1197, Port Townsend, WA 98368
360/385-2230 360/385-7785 Fax
www.loompanics.com   <editorial@loompanics.com>

We publish: books
Styles of fine art we tend to need: art with a message or
punch line to illustrate articles or books
Our target market is: readers of books considered unusual or
controversial
Types of artwork you hire free-lancers for: book covers,
article illustrations
We are: actively seeking illustrators, reviewing unsolicited
work from fine artists
Artists can contact us by: e-mailing portfolio
Best time of year to submit portfolio: anytime
We prefer to review: postcard
Tips for those contacting us: Keep it simple. An e-mail
address for contact. A web site is a fine way to show us
your work.

Meadowbrook Press

Peggy Bates
5451 Smetana Dr, Minnetonka, MN 55343
952/930-1100 952/930-1940 Fax

We publish: books
Styles of fine art we tend to need: varies
Our target market is: parents, adults, children, humor, party, infant
Types of artwork you hire freelancers for: cover and interior art
We are: actively seeking illustators, reviewing unsolicited work from fine artists
Artists can contact us by: submitting non-returnable portfolio for review by mail
We prefer to review: samples to keep

Modern Publishing

Edward Lenk
155 E 55th St, New York, NY 10022
212/826-0850 212/759-9069 Fax
www.modernpublishing.com
<elenk@modernpublishing.com>

Mondo

Don Curry
980 Avenue of the Americas, New York, NY 10018
212/268-3560
www.mondopub.com   <currydl@aol.com>

We publish: books
Styles of fine art we tend to need: variety
Our target market is: picture books and juvenile novels
Types of artwork you hire free-lancers for: picture book illustration
We are: actively seeking fine artists, actively seeking illustrators, seeking artists through referral, reviewing unsolicited work from fine artists, filing slides for possible future work
Artists can contact us by: submitting portfolio for review by mail, e-mailing portfolio
We prefer to review: photoprints, bio
Tips for those contacting us: Send a broad sampling of work. If you want something returned, send a SASE.

Oregon Catholic Press

Jean Germano
5536 NE Hassalo, Portland, OR 97213
503/281-1191
www.ocp.org

We publish: books, records
Types of artwork you hire freelancers for: cover design
We are: reviewing unsolicited work from fine artists
Artists can contact us by: submitting portfolio for review by mail, e-mailing portfolio
We prefer to review: photoprints

Peachtree Publishers

Loraine Joyner
1700 Chattahoochee Ave, Atlanta, GA 30318-2112

We publish: books
Contact person: Melanie McMahon or Loraine Joyner
Styles of fine art we tend to need: painterly, realistic fine art
Our target market is: children, young adults
Types of artwork you hire free-lancers for: book jackets, picture books, interior illustration
We are: reviewing unsolicited work from fine artists
Artists can contact us by: submitting portfolio for review by mail
We prefer to review: color copies
Tips for those contacting us: only send via postal service, not via e-mail

Random House Children's Books

Jan Gerardi
1540 Broadway, New York, NY 10036
212/782-8408 212/782-9698
www.randomhouse.com/kids

We publish: books
Styles of fine art we tend to need: realistic as well as stylized, but not abstract. Should be suitable for children's books.
Our target market is: children - 12 years
We are: actively seeking illustrators,
Artists can contact us by: submitting samples for review by mail (no originals)
Best time of year to submit portfolio: anytime
We prefer to review: color printouts, photoprints
Tips for those contacting us: Send samples for children's books; art that can be kept on file. Do not send original art.

Spartacus Publishing

Casey C Clark
3906 Grace Ellen Dr, Columbia, MO 65202
573/474-1449 Fax
www.spartacuspublishing.com
<cclark@spartacuspublishing.com>

We publish: books
Styles of fine art we tend to need: B&W line art
Our target market is: 18-35
Types of artwork you hire free-lancers for: interior illustrations
We are: actively seeking illustrators
Artists can contact us by: submitting portfolio for review by mail
We prefer to review: photocopies
Tips for those contacting us: please be patient

The Speech Bin Inc

J Binney
1965 25th Ave, Vero Beach, FL 32960
www.speechbin.com

We publish: books
Styles of fine art we tend to need: B&W realistic illustrations
Our target market is: speech-language pathologists, special educators, rehab
Types of artwork you hire free-lancers for: books, games (educational)
We are: reviewing unsolicited work from artists with SASE
Artists can contact us by: submitting portfolio or letter with samples for review by mail
Best time of year to submit portfolio: anytime
We prefer to review: photoprints
Tips for those contacting us: SASE is a must

Stemmer House Publishers

Barbara Holdridge
2627 Caves Rd, Owings Mills, MD 21117
410/363-3690   410/363-8459 Fax
www.stemmer.com

We publish: books
Styles of fine art we tend to need: pictorial
Our target market is: children

Types of artwork you hire free-lancers for: books
We are: reviewing unsolicited work from fine artists
Artists can contact us by: submitting samples for review by mail
Best time of year to submit portfolio: Autumn
We prefer to review: photoprints
Tips for those contacting us: Enclose postcard with range of responses for quick check-off!

W Publishing Group

Tom Williams
545 Marriott Dr #750, Nashville, TN 37214
www.wpublishinggroup.com
<twilliams@wpublishinggroup.com>

We publish: books
Styles of fine art we tend to need: traditional styles
Our target market is: book readers
Types of artwork you hire free-lancers for: cover design and illustration
We are: actively seeking fine artists, actively seeking illustrators, reviewing unsolicited work from fine artists
Artists can contact us by: e-mailing portfolio
Best time of year to submit portfolio: anytime
We prefer to review: printed samples
Tips for those contacting us: No calls please. Use mail or e-mail.

Wright Group/McGraw-Hill

Chris Wangelin
PO Box 340, Flagstaff, AZ 86002-0340
800/523-2053   520/526-1967 Fax

We publish: books
Our target market is: educational, grade K-6
Types of artwork you hire free-lancers for: design, editing
We are: actively seeking illustrators
Artists can contact us by: submitting portfolio for review by mail, e-mailing portfolio
We prefer to review: photo prints
Tips for those contacting us: send SASE postcard

BOOK AND DIRECTORY PUBLISHERS

ArtNetwork
PO Box 1360, Nevada City, CA 95959
800/383-0677 530/470-0862 530/470-0256 Fax
www.artmarketing.com <info@artmarketing.com>
Teaching artists how to market since 1986. Books include (Art Marketing 101, Art Office), *newsletters* (ArtWorld Hotline, ArtSource Quarterly), *an on-line gallery, mailing lists of artworld professionals in over 25 categories (consultants, designers, publishers, licensing agents, calendar publishers, greeting card reps and more). Call for free brochure, which covers it all.*

A&C Black
Linda Lambert
37 Soho Sq, London W1D 3QZ England
0207/758-0200
www.acblack.com <llambert@acblack.com>
Publish Writers' and Artists' Yearbook—*a must if you want to find clients or an agent in England. It has a list of greeting card manufacturers, newspapers, magazines and children's book publishers. Approximately $18.*

A4 Publications Ltd
Galleon House, 35 Hagley Rd, Stourbridge, West Midlands, DY8 1QR England
www.a4publications.com
<jerry.woodbridge@a4publications.com>
This company produces a range of magazines to the trade (licensing agents, licensors and retail buyers) including The Art Buyer *and* Licensing Today Worldwide. *If you have a major success, ensure you get some good PR. Send an article and slides.*

Allworth Press
10 E 23rd St, New York, NY 10010
212/777-8395
www.allworth.com <pub@allworth.com>
Publishes legal books, among them Licensing Art & Design *by Caryn R Leland, for artists as well as a variety of other books, including web and marketing information.*

EPM Communications
Sean McDonald
160 Mercer St #3 Fl, New York, NY 10012-3212
212/941-0099
www.epmcom.com <smcdonald@epmcom.com>
Licensing Letter Sourcebook *is updated annually and has more than 35,000 listings of agents, consultants, manufacturers and others in the licensing industry. Several other publications also.*

F&W Publications
4700 E Galbraith Rd, Cincinnati, OH 45236-6190
800/289-0963 513/531-2222
Artist and Graphic Designers Market; Children's Writer's and Illustrator's Market; *and many more*

National Rep Group Directory
Spoor & Associates
2048 May Valley Wy, Henderson, NV 89052
800/770-7470
www.spoorconsultants.com
$100; updated annually, includes producers of trade shows, industry associations, trade publications, national reps of gifts, toys, gourmet products and decorative accessories

Thomas Registry of American Manufacturers
1 Penn Plz, New York, NY 10001
212/695-0500
Go to a library to review this immense 12-volume directory. You will find listings of over 65,000 companies by the product they manufacturer. If you know the type of product you want to put your work on, this is a great reference source.

COMPUTER SOFTWARE

MarketingArtist
www.marketingartist.com
Easy and intuitive online business management software for artists, powered by LiveWire. Can use from Mac or PC. Mailing list management, artwork and exhibition documentation and more. Free until certain quantity of usage; then only $9.95 per month.

Spinnsoft
Doug Spinn
877/568-0707   949/707-0777
www.spinnsoft.com   <doug@spinnsoft.com>
Spinnsoft produces easy-to-use software tools to increase sales and efficiency and decrease frustration. Spinnsoft includes inventory control, invoicing and financial reporting, web site updating and more.

CONSULTANTS

Art Licensing International Inc
Michael Woodward
1532 US 41 Bypass S #272, Venice FL 34293-1032
941/488-8464   941/488-8454 Fax
www.artlicensinginc.com   <michaelwoodward@mac.com>
Member of LIMA. Author of Art Licensing 101. *Licensing consultant for artwork collections*

ArtNetwork
Constance Smith
530/470-0862
www.artmarketing.com/consulting
<info@artmarketing.com>
A telephone-based consulting service that will help you answer all your art marketing and licensing questions. Author of Art Marketing 101.

Todd Bingham
1016 Eucalyptus Ave, Vista, CA 92084
760/806-7699   760/806-9622
www.tbfa.com   <mo@tbfa.com>
Does consulting by e-mail and phone with artists and galleries

The Licensing Department
Ronnie Pollack
8952 Dicks St, Los Angeles, CA 90069
310/275-5337
www.licensingconsultant.com   <agentrp@aol.com>

LAWYERS

Cowan, DeBaets, Abrams & Sheppard
Mitchell Radin
212/974-7474
<mradin@cdas.com>

Feldman Law Firm
12 E 41st St, New York, NY 10017
212/532-8585
www.feldman-law.com   <sfeldman@feldman-law.com>

Freeborn & Peters
Eugene Zelek
312/360-6777
www.freebornpeters.com   <ezelek@freebornpeters.com>

Grimes and Battersby
Gregory Battersby
203/324-2828

The Intellectual Property Group
Jamie Silverberg, John Mason
1501 M St Northwest #1150, Washington, DC 20005
202/466-2787
www.artlaws.com   <artlaws@aol.com>

J Turner & Associates
310/273-4858
www.turner-law.com   <ljturner@turner-law.com>

Lawrence Turner
310/273-4858
www.turner-law.com <ljturner@turner-law.com>

Offner & Anderson
Daniel Offner
310/226-2420
www.offneranderson.com <doffner@offneranderson.com>

Paula Grafstein-Suarez
631/425-2702
<pgrafsteinsuarez@aol.com>

Licensing and trademark, copyright matters

Rebecca Stroder
Spencer, Fane, Britt & Browne LLP
1000 Walnut Street #1400, Kansas City, MO 64106
816/292-8301
<rstroder@spencerfane.com>

Venable, Baetjer, Howard & Civiletti
Joshua Kaufman
1201 New York Ave NW #1000, Washington, DC 20005
202/962-4800
www.jjkaufman.com <jjkaufman@venable.com>
Intellectual property specialist

Wragge & Co
Gordon Harris
England
44/121-233-1000
www.wragge.com
Specialist in European trademark and intellectual property law

LEGAL ORGANIZATIONS

American Arbitration Association
212/484-4000

Aspen Law Publishers
1185 Ave of the Americas, New York, NY 10036
800/638-8437 800/234-1660
www.aspenpublishers.com
This company publishes a variety of books related to the licensing industry: The Trademark Handbook, The Licensing Library, Trademark Law & The Patent Practice Handbook *plus more.*

www.lawyers.com
This web site will help you to locate a specific type of lawyer. (For publishing and licensing legalities you want an intellectual property specialist). All you have to do is type in your state and city, together with "Intellectual property/Trademarks" to locate a local specialist. Lawyers in big cities such as New York, Los Angeles, Washington and Chicago usually have more experience in this type of work.

Volunteer Lawyers for the Arts/VLA
1 E 53rd St #6Fl, New York, NY 10022
212/319-2787
www.artswire.org/artlaw/info.html
This is the main office—there are many branches in major cities across the US. You can go on-line to find one near you.

Ft Mason, Bldg C-255, San Francisco, CA 94123
415/775-7000

251 S 18th St, Philadelphia, PA 19103 215/545-3385
They have a list of all the VLA organizations across the nation.

MAGAZINES

You can usually get a free review copy by calling the subscription department.

Lists of art magazines can be found at:
www.artmarketing.com/Links/a_pub.html

Accessories Magazine
Business Journals Inc
50 Day St, Norwalk, CT 06856
203/853-6015

Accessory Merchandising
847/634-2600

American Craft
72 Spring St, New York, NY 10012-4019
212/274-0630

Apparel Merchandising
425 Park Ave, New York, NY 10022
212/756-5134

Art Business News
1 Park Avenue #2Fl, New York, NY 10016-5802
218/723-9477   888/527-7008 (subscriptions)
www.artbusinessnews.com
A must for anyone wanting to get into fine art publishing

Art Business Today
16-18 Empress Place, London SW6 1TT England
011/44-207-381-6616
Magazine for print and framing market published by the Fine Art Trade Guild

Art Expressions
Kerkstraat 14, 3632 El, Loenen AAN De Vecht, Netherlands
011/31-294-232-908
<artexpressions@wxs.nl>
International art and framing industry magazine

Art Trends
225 Gordons Corner Rd, Manapalan, NJ 07726
800/969-7176
The magazine of fine art prints

Art World News
887 E Wilmette Rd #C-2, Palatine, IL 60067
847/705-6519
www.artworldnews.com   <jbmale@aol.com>
$6 for a single issue

Brandweek
PO Box 1973, Danbury, CT 06813
800/722-6658
www.brandweek.com

Decor
330 N 4th St, St Louis, MO 63102
314/421-5445
Many publishers advertise in this magazine, so you can study what types and styles of artwork they print.

Digital Fine Art Magazine
51 Madison Ave, New York, NY 10010
212/689-4411
www.digitalfineart.com

Giclée
PO Box 420
Manalpan, NJ 07726-0420

Gift & Decorative Accessories
345 Hudson St #4Fl, New York, NY 10014
212/519-7200   800/309-3332 (subscriptions)
www.giftanddec.com   www.cahners.com
Also publishes Gayer's Dealer Topics, Buyers Guide, Playthings Magazine *and* Playthings Directory, Who Makes It and Where

Gift and Stationery Business
1 Penn Plz, New York, NY 10019-0004
212/714-1300

Gift and Tablewares
1450 Don Mills Rd, Don Mills, Ontario Canada
416/422-2068
www.gifts-and-tablewares.com

Giftware News
20 N Wacker Dr #1865, Chicago, IL 60600
800/229-1967 ext 50   312/849-2220
www.giftwarenews.net
$5 for sample issue

Greetings
4 Middlebury Blvd, Randolph, NJ 07869-1111
973/252-0100   973/252-0100 (subscriptions)
www.edgellcommunications.com
<tmccarthy@edgellmail.com>
The magazine for the greeting card and stationery market. Also publishes Selling Christmas Decorations.

Home Accents Today
800/395-2329

Home Décor Buyer
847/675-7400

Home Furnishings News
7 W 34th St, New York, NY 10001
800/424-8698

Home Textiles Today
245 W 17th St, New York, NY 10011
212/337-6906   800/395-2329 (subscriptions)

How
800/289-0963   513/531-2222
This magazine has articles on book illustration and design.

Informart
Westtown Publishing
PO Box 147, Easton, CT 06612
203/268-5552
www.informartmag.com   <peggy@informartmag.com>

License! Magazine
1 Park Ave, New York, NY 10016
888/527-7008   888/527-7008 (subscriptions)
www.advanstar.com   <atambini@advanstar.com>
Publish a supplement called The Art of Licensing *as well as a* Sourcebook

The Licensing Book
1501 Broadway #500, New York, NY 10036
212/575-4510
www.licensingbook.com   <mscheiner@licensingbook.com>

The Licensing Journal
PO Box 1169, Stamford, CT 06904-1169
203/358-0848

The Licensing Letter
160 Mercer St #3Fl, New York, NY 10012
212/941-0099
<epmcommun@aol.com>
Also publishes The Licensing Business Handbook *by Karen Raugust*

Licensing Trends
51 Madison Ave, New York, NY 10010

Licensing Wire
www.licensingworld.com
An on-line newsletter: $49.95 for one year; $26.95 for six months

Picture Business
Greater London House, Hampstead Rd, London England NW1 7EJ
011/44-20-7391-3300
<picturebusiness@fashion.emag.co.uk>
Trade magazine for the fine art publishing business

Publishers Weekly
245 W 17th St, New York, NY 10011
212/463-6758
This magazine will keep you abreast of new books, calendars and cover designs. $6.50 per issue

Sunshine Artist
3210 Dade Ave, Orlando, FL 32804
407/228-9772
Outdoor art show listings—places to sell your prints

MAILING LISTS

ArtNetwork
PO Box 1360, Nevada City, CA 95959-1360
800/38309677
Art publishers, licensing agents, calendar publishers, greeting card publishers, print distributors, galleries, consultants, reps, dealers, brokers, museum curators, museum store buyers, interior designers, architects, corporate collections and more, all on pressure-sensitive labels, the easy peel-and-stick type! For counts and prices, call for a free brochure.

www.bigroster.com

Steve Langerman Lists
207/761-2116
Record company lists and more

MERCHANDISE MARTS

AmericasMart Atlanta
240 Peachtree St NW, Atlanta, Georgia 30303
800/285-6278   404/220-3000

Chicago Merchandise Mart
312/527-7600
www.merchandisemart.com
Fairs in Feb and July

Dallas Trade Mart
2100 Stemmons Freeway, Dallas, TX 75207
214/760-2852

Denver Merchandise Mart
451 E 58th St, Denver, CO 80216
303/292-6278
Shows in Feb and August

Los Angeles Merchandise Mart
1933 S Broadway, Los Angeles, CA 90014
213/749-7911

New York Mart
230 Fifth Ave, New York, NY 10010
212/532-4555

San Francisco Gift Mart
1355 Market St, San Francisco, CA 94103
415/552-2311

ORGANIZATIONS

Alliance for the Arts
330 W 42 St #1701, New York, NY 10036
212/947-5340
www.allianceforarts.org

American Booksellers Association
828 S Broadway, Tarrytown, NY 10591
914/591-2665
Sponsor Book Expo America each year in June

American Institute of Graphic Arts
164 Fifth Ave, New York, NY 10010
212/807-1990

Americans for the Arts
1 E 53 St, New York, NY 10022
212/223-2787

Artists Rights Society/ARS
536 Broadway #5Fl, New York, NY 10012
212/420-9160
www.arsny.com
Represents artists in publishing, licensing and copyright matters

Association of American Publishers
71 Fifth Ave, New York, NY 10003
212/225-0200

Association of the Graphic Arts Communications
Diane Chavon
330 Seventh Ave #9Fl, New York, NY 10001
212/279-2100 ext 109
www.agcomm.org <dchavan@agcomm.org>

Calendar Advertising Council
PO Box 15092, Austin, TX 78761
512/323-0735

Calendar Market Association
Dick Mikes
710 E Ogden Ave #600, Naperville, IL 60563
630/579-3264 630/369-2488 Fax
www.calendarmarketplace.com <cma@b-online.com>
Call or write for information on the many items this association offers. They publish a book—How to Publish/Market Your Calendar @ *$69.95 + shipping.*

Fine Art Trade Guild
16-18 Empress Place, London SW6 1TT England
44/207-381-6616
www.fineart.co.uk
Marketing trade organization for publishers of fine art, galleries and framers

Giclée Printers Association/GPA
714/279-2312
<rjcoulston@harvestpro.com>

Graphic Arts Guild
90 John Street, New York, NY 10038-3202
800/500-2672
www.gag.org
The main union for illustrators and artists, particularly for those in advertising, book jacket design, magazine illustration. Publishers of the very useful guide to ethics and business practices for artists—Pricing and Ethical Guidelines.

Graphic Arts Association
1100Northbrook Dr #120, Trevose, PA 19053-8404

The Greeting Card Association
1156 15th St NW #900, Washington, DC 20005
202/393·1778
www.greetingcard.org
The information available through this association is invaluable.

Licensing Industry Merchandising Association/LIMA
350 Fifth Ave #2309, New York, NY 10118
212/244-1944
www.licensing.org
This is the main licensing organization in the US. They have a very useful web site that lists information about licensing as well as agents. Membership provides access to a broad variety of activities, information, sources and benefits. Publishes the Licensing Resource Directory: Who's Who in the Licensing Industry

The Professional Artists Association
www.profineart.com

New York Artists Equity Association/NYAEA
498 Broome St, New York, NY 10013
212/941-0130
www.anny.org

Society of Illustrators
128 E 63rd St, New York, NY 10021
212/838-2560

Society of Photographers and Artists Representatives/SPAR
60 E 42nd St #1166, New York, NY 10165

Visual Artists' and Galleries' Association/VAGA
350 Fifth Ave #6305, New York, NY 10118
212/736-6666 212/736-6767 Fax
<info@vagarights.com>

PRINTERS

Colson Printing
711 N Oak St, Valdosta, GA 31601-4599
800/323-7280   229/242-7015
www.colsonprint.com <art@colsonprint.com>
Full-service color printer specializing in fine art lithographs and giclées. Free art information kit available.

Color Q
2710 Dryden Rd, Dayton, OH 45439
800/999-1007 513/294-0406

Mitchell Graphics
Josh
2363 Mitchell Park Dr, Petosky, MI 49770
800/583-9405
www.mitchellgraphics.com <joshw@mitchellgraphics.com>
We've used them to print postcards. Excellent customer service and good, timely printing.

Coupralux
Krista Jasper/Gallery Director
1616-C Hi Line Dr, Dallas TX 75207
214/760-0077 214/760-0080
www.coupralux.com <bowers@coupralux.com>
An Iris giclée service bureau, they also have a gallery selling artwork from the artists they print. Web site development.

PSPress
2861 Mandela Pkwy, Oakland, CA 94608
800/511-2009 510/444-3933
www.psprint.com <info@psprint.com>
A postcard printer

ROYALTY COMPLIANCE AUDITS

Licensing Financial Srvices Inc
Paul Brachie
1023 Paxton Ave, Cincinnati, OH 45208
513/871-7938 513/871-7948 Fax
<brachie@superm.com>

TRADE SHOW ORGANIZERS

Advancestar Communications
7500 Old Oak Blvd, Cleveland, OH 44130
800/827-7170 www.artexpos.com www.advanstar.com
Licensing Show (NY); Licensing Europe (Germany), Brand Licensing London (October), ArtExpoNY (March), ArtExpoSF (November)

George Little Management
10 Bank St, White Plains, NY 10606
914/421-3200
www.glmshows.com

TRADE SHOWS

www.tsnn.com
Offers listings of every trade show in the world including the number of exhibitors, exhibition floor space and attendees

American International Toy Fair
Toy Industry Association
1115 Broadway, New York NY 10010
212/675 -1141
www.toy-tma.com/aitf <toyfairs@toy-tia.org>
Held in February in New York City

Art Atlanta
216/328-8926
www.art-atlanta.com
May

ArtExpo
Advancestar Communications
800/322-5226
www.artexpos.com
*The New York ArtExpo, held in March each year, is
by far the biggest show of its kind in the US. It is
possible for fine artists to take booth space to sell
originals and limited-edition prints. A show is also
held in California in November and Miami in
January.*

Book Expo
American Booksellers Association
828 S Broadway, Tarrytown, NY 10591
914/591-2665
www.bookexpoamerica.com

Boston Gift Show
George Little Management
914/421-3200
March and September

Brand Licensing Show
Advanstar Communications
800/827-7170
www.licensingshow.com <mwkelly@advanstar.com>
*The main event in UK for licensing concepts, TV-
based properties and art. Held in Oct at the
Business Design Center in London.*

Dallas International Gift & Home Accessories
George Little Management
914/421-3200
Held in January

Decor Expos
330 N 4th St, St Louis, MO 63102
314/421-5445
www.decormagazine.com
*These shows are for exhibiting reproductions to the
print trade. Long Beach, CA, Jan; Orlando, FL,
Feb; New York, March; Dallas, April*

Florida Gift Show
404/220-2200
Feb, April

International Housewares Show/NHMA
110 W Hubbard St, Chicago, IL 60610
800/752-1052
www.housewares.org/ihshow
Held at McCormick Place in Chicago in January

**International Exhibition of Stationery, Paper and
Cardboard Products/CART**
Fiera Milano International SpA
Largo Domodossola 1, 20145 Milano, Italy
www.fmi.it
Held in January

Licensing Europe
www.licensingeurope.net
Held in Munich in September

Licensing International
Advanstar
203/882-1300
www.licensingshow.com
*LIMA sponsors the worlds largest trade show and
conference for licensing professionals. The
International Licensing Show is a three-day event
each June at the Jacob Javitts Center in New York
City; meet with licensing agents; network with key
executives in the business, and attend seminars and
conferences. Show exhibitors are licensing agents
representing more than 5,000 properties, including
characters, trademarks, original designs,
entertainment, sports, animation, personalities and
more. The LIMA 2001 Licensing University Programs
featured over 15 sessions focusing on all facets of the
licensing industry. This is THE show for licensing
executives who travel from all over the globe to see and
be seen at this once-a-year showplace of the cutting edge
of licensing creativity. Major art licensing section
available for artists and agents.*

Licensing World
www.licensingworld.com
*Trade show is held annually in January in
Frankfurt, Germany. Their web site has useful
information on licensing in general. Also has an on-
line newsletter called* LicensingWire.

National Stationery Show
George Little Management
800/222-SHOW
www.glmshows.com <info@glmshows.com>
Held in mid-May in New York City. A major event covering gifts, stationery, greeting cards and many other products. Held congruently with Surtex.

New York Home Textiles Show
George Little Management
800/222-SHOW
Surtex Gallery features the newest in art and design for every home fashion product. Held mid-October.

New York International Gift Fair
George Little Management
800/222-SHOW
Held in January at the Jacob Javits Center in New York City

Philadelphia Gift Show
610/272-4024
January, July

San Francisco International Gift Fair
George Little Management
800/222-SHOW

Spring Fair
Trade Promotion Services Ltd
19th Floor, Leon House, High Street, Croydon England
44/208-277-5863
www.springfair.com <info@tps.emap.co.uk>
Held at the National Exhibition Centre/NEC in Birmingham, England in February. A major event covering fine art publishing, greeting cards, gift products, housewares, stationery, etc.

Surtex
George Little Management
914/421-3200
www.surtex.com
To show surface design artwork. This show allows you to license your work directly to manufacturers. Held in May, concurrently with the National Stationery Show in New York City.

WEB SITES

It's best to do a search for a specific topic you need information on.

Licensing World
www.licensingworld.com
Lists licensing agents. This is a privately owned enterprise of a small group of experienced licensing professionals. Costs $499 a year to be listed in their gallery: 7 art pieces and 500 words.

The Art of Licensing
groups.yahoo.com/group/TheArtofLicensing
A web site where artists from beginners to the most experienced can share their knowledge in the area of licensing art and design to manufacturers and publishers. A great place to share ideas, tips and techniques.

www.GiftBusiness.com
Wholesale gift industry resource; free information resources and advertising for reps wanted, lines wanted and a marktplace page for miscellaneous ads. Gift Industries Web Yellow Pages, an online source for publications gift marts, manufactuer's representatives and gift industry associations. Gift Trade Marketing, A Beginners Handbook is sold for $18.95.

www.AmericasGiftShow.com
National trade show that exhibits to retail buyers directly. Cost to exhibit an image for six months is $80.

www.artmarketing.com

www.absolutearts.com

www.art-posters-prints.com

www.artpublishers.org

www.licensingcourse.com

NOTES

NOTES

NOTES

Art Office

80⁺

This book provides artists with a wide selection of indispensable business forms, charts, sample letters, legal documents and business plans . . . all for photocopying. Organize your office's administrative and planning functions. Reduce routine paperwork and increase time for your art creation.

Forms include:

12-month planning calendar ❧ Sales agreement
Model release ❧ Rental-lease agreement ❧ Form VA
Slide reference sheet ❧ Competition record
Customer-client record ❧ Phone-zone sheet
Monthly project status form ❧ Marketing plan
12-month show planner ❧ Checklist for a juried show
Print planning calendar ❧ Bill of sale
Pricing work sheet ❧ Press release ❧ and lots more

ABOUT THE AUTHORS
Sue Viders has been a practicing artist and art consultant for over 30 years. **Constance Smith** founded ArtNetwork over 16 years ago to assist artists nationwide with their marketing.

$15.95   112 pages   ISBN: 0-940899-27-2

ArtNetwork
530·470·0862   800·383·0677   530·470·0256 Fax
PO Box 1360, Nevada City, CA 95959-1360
www.artmarketing.com   <info@artmarketing.com>

Come see our body of work

Your web page with ArtNetwork will include five reproductions of your artwork (example at right). Each artwork clicks onto an enlarged rendition, approximately three times the size. Two hundred words of copy (whatever you want to say) are allowed.

Our site averages 700 users a day (and going up each quarter), with the gallery being the second most visited area on our site (the first is our main page).

☞ We publicize our site to art publishers, gallery owners, museum curators, consultants, architects, interior designers and more! We receive over 175,000 hits per month. Your home page on our site will be seen by important members of the art world.

☞ You will have an address that will take your customers directly to your artwork. Your address will have your name in it, i.e., **www.artmarketing.com/gallery/johndoe**

☞ You will want to put this web address on business cards, letterhead, envelopes, brochures, flyers, and any advertising you do. Tell the world where you live on the Internet so they will come see what you do!

To showcase your artwork on-line send:

Five images for ArtNetwork to scan; a combination of horizontal and vertical is fine. You can send photo prints/35mm slides/jpgs. Note on slides "top front." If you send a photo/print, it can be no smaller than 2x2 ", no larger than 8x10 ". Artwork is electronically scanned and reproduced, using 72 dpi resolution. No color corrections are made, so send well-taken pieces.

A list of the five images: title, size, medium, retail price, and if prints are available, cost and size of prints.

Check, money order or charge card number (VISA/MC/AmExpress/Discover): $160 for two years of service; $115 for one year.

Legible copy of no more than 200 words.

E-mail address

A #10 SASE for return of your materials

ArtNetwork
530·470·0862   800·383·0677   530·470·0256 Fax
PO Box 1360, Nevada City, CA 95959-1360
www.artmarketing.com   <info@artmarketing.com>

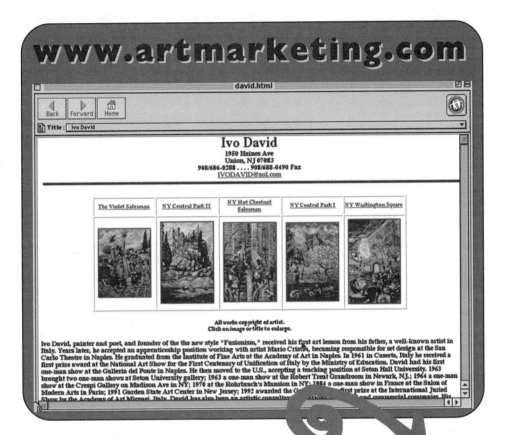

Surfing our site

- Visit our 600-page site at www.artmarketing.com

- Visit over 90 artists at www.artmarketing.com/gallery

- Browse to our book section and find articles to improve your marketing techniques at www.artmarketing.com/101

- At www.artmarketing.com/Homepg/hotlinks.html you will find leads to residencies, grants, lawyers, consultants, organizations, art fairs, licensing agents, art magazines, museums, galleries, resources and art supplies of all types, info about taxes, special travel adventures for artists and much, much more!

- Sign up in our guestbook and receive a free article about promoting your site.

- Find a local art fair to attend with our search engine at bottom of page at www.artmarketing.com.

ArtNetwork

530·470·0862   800·383·0677   530·470·0256 Fax

PO Box 1360, Nevada City, CA 95959-1360

www.artmarketing.com   <info@artmarketing.com>

Living Artists

In this competitive and fast-paced world, an artist needs to take marketing seriously. Here's a way to do it dynamically and economically! *Living Artists* (formerly titled the *Encyclopedia of Living Artists*) is a direct link to prime customers—including reps, corporate art consultants, gallery owners, interior designers , museum curators and more. These artworld professionals use this book to select artwork throughout the year for various projects. Artwork in the book is reproduced in high-quality, full-color, along with artist's name, address and telephone number. Prospective buyers have direct contact with the artist of choice. All fine artists are invited to submit their work; a maximum of 75 artists are chosen for publication. Published biannually in odd-numbered years. A contest is conducted for the cover position.

> **3500** galleries **1000** consultants and reps **150** corporate art consultants **450** museum curators **400** interior designers **425** architects **1000** college gallery directors **500** embassies, health clinics, bed and breakfasts **200** public art agencies **200** collectors **175** corporations collecting art

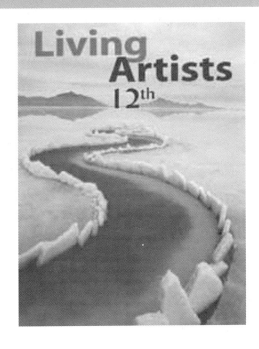

ArtNetwork
530·470·0862   800·383·0677   530·470·0256 Fax
PO Box 1360, Nevada City, CA 95959-1360
www.artmarketing.com   <info@artmarketing.com>

Mailing Lists

		PRICE PER LIST
1.	41,000 Visual Artists	$100 per 1000
2.	1000 Art Councils	$75
3.	350 Art Publications	$50
4.	1750 Art Publishers	$130*
4A.	900 Greeting Card Publishers	$70
4B.	125 Print Distributors	$40
4C.	400 Greeting Card Sales Reps	$50
4D.	240 Licensing Contacts	$50
4E.	160 Calendar Publishers	$40
5.	400 Book Publishers	$50
6.	600 Corporations Collecting Art	$70
6A.	180 Corporations Collecting Photography	$40
7.	750 Art Stores	$60
8.	2000 Reps, Consultants, Dealers, Brokers	$140*
8A.	140 Corporate Art Consultants	$55
9.	1900 College Art Departments	$140*
9A.	1900 College Galleries	$140*
10.	600 Libraries	$60
11.	6500 Galleries	$75 per 1000*
11A.	500 Photo Galleries	$55
11B.	800 New York Galleries	$65
12.	600 Foreign Galleries	$90
12B.	300 Canadian Galleries	$50
13.	2000 Art Organizations and Exhibition Spaces	$140*
13A.	490 Art Organization Newsletters	$65
14.	900 Art Museums	$75
14A.	540 Art Museum Store Buyers	$75
15.	800 Architects	$50
16.	750 Interior Designers	$50
17.	2000 Frame and Poster Galleries	$140*

All lists can be rented for onetime use and may not be copied, duplicated or reproduced in any form. Lists have been seeded to detect unauthorized usage. Reorder of same lists within a 12-month period qualifies for 25% discount. Lists cannot be returned or exchanged.

FORMATS/CODING

All domestic names are provided in zip code sequence on three-up pressure-sensitive labels. We mail to each company/person on our list a minimum of once per year. Our business thrives by responses to our mailings, so we keep them as up-to-date and clean as we possibly can.

SHIPPING

Please allow one week for processing your order once your payment has been received. Lists are sent priority mail and take an additional 2-4 days. Orders sent without shipping costs will be delayed.

GUARANTEE

Each list is guaranteed 95% deliverable. We will refund 37¢ per piece for undeliverable mail in excess of 5% if returned to us within 90 days of order.

ArtNetwork
530·470·0862   800·383·0677   530·470·0256 Fax
PO Box 1360, Nevada City, CA 95959-1360
www.artmarketing.com   <info@artmarketing.com>

Newsletters

Blast off to success!

Published every three months, this eight-page newsletter is packed full of new ideas (and no advertising)
that will give your art business the creative edge, taking your sales to new levels. Subscribe to *ArtSource Quarterly* for the most current marketing information.

- Innovative marketing ideas
- Hot tips
- Interviews with successful artists
- Articles by artworld professionals

Subscription Rates

4 issues (1 year)	$19
8 issues (2 years)	$34
Current issue	$ 6

"I really love your quarterly newsletter. Your hot tips are great. I saved the cost of one year's subscription on products I needed and found through your publication. Thanks!"

NW, Artist, Washington

Monthly listings

With *ArtWorld Hotline* you'll receive 40-60 **new** listings each month—listings not found in any other publication—opportunities
to advance your career.
This four-page monthly includes:

- Gallery calls • Grants
- Consultants needing artwork
- Publishers seeking artwork
- Residencies • Shows
- Competitions • Exhibitions
- and many more unique listings

"I received an exhibition in the Senate Rotunda in Washington, DC, thanks to you."

FF, Artist, Connecticut

Subscription Rates

12 issues (1 year)	$26
24 issues (2 years)	$48
Current issue	$ 3

ArtNetwork
530·470·0862   800·383·0677   530·470·0256 Fax
PO Box 1360, Nevada City, CA 95959-1360
www.artmarketing.com   <info@artmarketing.com>

ArtFolio

Publishers are constantly seeking new and innovative artwork for posters, greeting cards, limited-edition prints, calendars and licensing opportunities. This 6x6" spiral-bound booklet, printed on heavy postcard stock, is the smartest way for artists to contact these publishers. ArtFolio exposes 98 artists to over 4000 art publishers for only $499! Published biannually in even-numbered years; deadline for application is May 30 of odd-numbered years.

900 greeting card publishers **180** licensing companies **170** calendar publishers **1800** art publishers **400** book publishers **370** greeting card reps **100** print distributors

ArtNetwork
530·470·0862   800·383·0677   530·470·0256 Fax
PO Box 1360, Nevada City, CA 95959-1360
www.artmarketing.com   <info@artmarketing.com>

Art Marketing 101

Learn how to gain exposure as a fine artist. Read about myths many artists fall prey to and how to avoid them. Identify roadblocks to success. You'll learn about:

* **Preparing a portfolio**
* **Pricing your work**
* **Alternative venues for selling your artwork**
* **Publishing and licensing**
* **Taking care of legal matters**
* **Developing a marketing plan**
* **Publicity matters**
* **Succeeding without a rep**
* **Secrets of successful artists**

amazon.com gives this book a five-star rating!

Learn what art schools don't teach: **business savvy**. No other book offers artists such concise step-by-step marketing strategies. This book answers such questions as:

* Must I depend on dealers, curators and gallery owners—or can I do it on my own?

* How do I protect my work from plagiarism?

This comprehensive 24-chapter volume covers all the key issues any artist needs to know to do business in today's world and includes:

* Case histories and success stories

* Detailed index

* Recommended reading lists

* Checklists to help you stay on track

* "Action Plan" at the end of each chapter

Experts say:

"How much time, money and heartache could have been saved had I had a copy of Art Marketing 101 *years ago. At last the fog has lifted!"*

Patricia George, Artist, California

"Absolutely everything artists need to know in order to sell their creative work in today's competitive marketplace. Full of excellent tips, practical information and reference material. A must for every artist who wants to make more money."

Sue Viders, Art Marketing Consultant, Colorado

"I highly recommend this book for beginning, emerging and established artists as a reference source for many different topics, as well as for an emotional support."

Synthia Saint James, Artist, California

$24.95   336 pages   ISBN: 0-940899-32-9

ArtNetwork
530·470·0862   800·383·0677   530·470·0256 Fax
PO Box 1360, Nevada City, CA 95959-1360
www.artmarketing.com   <info@artmarketing.com>